"Interpersonal conflict is a misery maker, stirring up chaos and the fog of war. Robert Jones carefully walks down the narrow road that makes peace and stirs up joy. His presentation is judicious, wide-ranging, balanced, biblical, and full of grace. Every counselor needs to know these things. Every struggler willing to take the time will benefit—and we are all strugglers in these matters. Speed-reading not allowed! *Pursuing Peace* needs to be slowly absorbed and would make a marvelous twelve-week study."

David Powlison, executive director, Christian Counseling & Educational Foundation; senior editor, *Journal of Biblical Counseling*

"Conflict comes in many shapes and sizes, so we need a variety of perspectives and insights into how to respond to it in biblically faithful ways. I am delighted that Robert Jones has brought his many years of pastoral and counseling experience to bear on this topic—providing a fresh perspective on how to approach conflict and estranged people in a grace-filled, gospel-centered way."

Ken Sande, president, Relational Wisdom 360; author, *The Peacemaker*

"In a day when 'us and them' seems to be the default presumption with which our society confronts culture, politics, and religion, Robert Jones has provided us a scripturally sound and pragmatic path to follow to experience the peace for which most of us have a God-given desire. While the book may find itself in the syllabus of many Christian counseling classes, it is equally at home in the school of practical theology. Rich with biblical references and connected to practical application, *Pursuing Peace* will be helpful specifically for those dealing with issues of conflict in any arena of life, and generally for all who wish to gain a clearer understanding of how to interact with others in God-pleasing ways. With uncanny insights and sharp clarity, Dr. Jones addresses and then makes sense of normal, everyday conflicts and how they should be handled so that full resolution might be experienced. This book is indeed a helpful contribution to the culture of our day."

Thom S. Rainer, president and CEO, LifeWay Christian Resources

"Robert Jones has written a most profitable and sound book in *Pursuing Peace*. Though I wish it were not needed in the church today, the fact is that the message and advice of this book are desperately needed even among believers. I urge all of God's leaders in the household of faith not only to read this volume, but to discuss it as a guide for what to do the next time the peace of Christ's church is disturbed. Such reading and discussion will save loads of grief and some future headaches, as well as possible loss of the joy of the Lord."

Walter C. Kaiser Jr., president emeritus, Gordon-Conwell Theological Seminary

"Conflicts in relationship are inevitable. However, they do not have to be destructive. *Pursuing Peace* is a faithful, biblical guide that shows us how we can actually grow and mature spiritually, and find grace and peace on the other side. This valuable resource will well serve the body of Christ."

Daniel L. Akin, president, Southeastern Baptist Theological Seminary

"Sinful human beings live in a broken and fallen world full of unwanted opportunities for painful and destructive conflict. Dr. Jones's practical and biblical insights provide an excellent guide to navigate the realities of conflict in God-honoring and effective ways. This book is for everyone who struggles with the inevitable conflict that so deeply impacts our lives and relationships. *Pursuing Peace* promotes faith, hope, and love in the One who is the Prince of Peace. A must-read for every believer."

Judy Dabler, founder, Creative Conciliation; coauthor, *Peacemaking Women: Biblical Hope for Resolving Conflict*

"Robert Jones gives us both a grand, God's-eye view of conflict and a down-to-earth, practical roadmap for healing in our relationships. The big picture keeps us coming back to the gospel again and again for fresh grace and wisdom, and the practical guidance brings it all home to daily life. This book has helped me personally and will be a valuable resource to me as a pastor as I counsel others through conflicts with spouses, family members, and friends."

Mike Wilkerson, founder, Redemption Group Network

"You do not need to read this book if you never experience conflict or do not know anyone else that does. If, however, conflict is part of your experience—as it is for the rest of us—you *must* read this book. Dr. Jones's words are anchored in the words of Scripture, rich in the graces of Christ, and full of practical wisdom. This book will serve as a reliable guide to anyone interested in pursuing relational peace."

Heath Lambert, executive director, Association of Certified Biblical Counselors; author, *The Biblical Counseling Movement after Adams*

"*Pursuing Peace* is an excellent guide for helping people biblically resolve conflict and is greatly needed in our world of inevitable conflict."

Oletha Barnett, reconciliation director, Oak Cliff Bible Fellowship, Dallas, Texas; attorney at law

PURSUING
PEACE

PURSUING PEACE

A CHRISTIAN GUIDE TO HANDLING OUR CONFLICTS

ROBERT D. JONES

CROSSWAY®

WHEATON, ILLINOIS

Cover design and image: Josh Dennis
Interior design and typesetting: Lakeside Design Plus

First printing 2012
Printed in the United States of America

Trade paperback ISBN:	978-1-4335-3013-5
ePub ISBN:	978-1-4335-3016-6
PDF ISBN:	978-1-4335-3014-2
Mobipocket ISBN:	978-1-4335-3015-9

Library of Congress Cataloging-in-Publication Data
Jones, Robert D., 1959–
Pursuing peace : a Christian guide to handling our conflicts / Robert D. Jones.
    p. cm.
    Includes bibliographical references and index.
    ISBN 978-1-4335-3013-5 (tp)
    1. Conflict management—Religious aspects—Christianity.
2. Interpersonal relations—Religious aspects—Christianity.
3. Reconciliation—Religious aspects—Christianity. 4. Forgiveness—
Religious aspects—Christianity. 5. Peace—Religious aspects—Christianity.
I. Title.
BV4597.53.C58J66 2012
248.8'6—dc23   2012009968

Crossway is a publishing ministry of Good News Publishers.

CH   28   27   26   25   24   23   22

To my wife, Lauren,
and to my adult sons, Tim and Dan

"How good and pleasant it is
when brothers live together in unity!" (Ps. 133:1)

I am grateful to our Lord and to each of you,
my sister in Christ and my two brothers in Christ,
for the many years of peace and pleasure we have known
in Hurricane and Raleigh, the "good and pleasant"
blessing we have enjoyed together as God's
gracious gifts to the Jones family.

Contents

Preface

Why am I passionate about pursuing relational peace? Because relationships wither without it.

In 2004 my wife Lauren and I and our two sons moved to Raleigh, North Carolina, where I teach at nearby Southeastern Baptist Theological Seminary in Wake Forest. Having lived in apartments and then a church parsonage for nineteen years, we bought our first house. After looking at twenty-three options in two days, we settled on our top choice: roomy for our family foursome, modestly priced, and nestled in a traffic-free cul-de-sac. And to top it all off, it was situated on my ideal-sized property, a whopping .19 acres (yes, the decimal point is accurate; I figured I could handle mowing that size lawn, or paying a teen, when my sons moved out).

What we didn't bank on was the condition of that little lawn. It was a weedy mess, a field not of dreams but of orchard-grass clumps. One of my sons tells of a 2:00 a.m. return home only to discover, as his car approached the house, that our little yard was a late-night hot spot for local deer. (We've contemplated posting a "Weed Buffet" sign and charging our dear deer friends a $9.95 all-you-can-eat fee.)

What did we do? We added a truckload of topsoil, seeded it, and then did the various things that the experts recommended at the proper intervals—fertilizing, spreading lime, aerating, reseeding, and so forth. But the reseeding, we were warned, had to be preceded by another vital step. To sow grass seed on top of the weeds would yield little grass; we had to weed out the orchard grass.

Relational conflict is like that orchard grass. We long to grow relationships marked by trust and joy and goodwill and honesty, but as we pursue these we find patches of unreconciled conflict underneath. Few maladies plague our lives more than relational conflict. Whether in our homes, our workplaces, our schools, or even our churches, tensions continue and disputes quickly sprout. Conflicts happen in every relationship: husband and wife, parent and child, brother and sister,

11

supervisor and employee, church member and church member—the list goes on. As a young counseling student I once asked a doctoral mentor whether I was unusual for having more conflicts with my wife than with other people. He assured me that my experience was quite common. Conflicts can mark, and mar, many of our relationships, even the dearest ones.

So what should we do? Your decision to pick up this book tells me three things about you. First, you are experiencing conflict in your life (or someone you care about is). Second, you are honest enough to admit it. Third, you are humble enough, or desperate enough, to seek help.

This book has two simple goals: to provide you with a step-by-step process for pursuing peace in all your relationships and to give you a tool you can use to help others. I wish to provide a clear path down which you and your friends and family members can walk with confidence and hope. It's a *biblical* path, one that relies on the absolute authority, sufficiency, and life-giving power of God's Spirit-breathed Word. It's a *Christ-centered* path, one that depends on the forgiving and empowering grace of Jesus our Redeemer and one that imitates the life of Jesus our example. It's a *practical* path, one that provides concrete action steps, case examples, and suggested language to handle specific situations. And it's a *proven* path, one that God has enabled me to follow in my life (albeit imperfectly), and one down which I have had the privilege of leading many hundreds of individuals, couples, churches, and Christians schools for nearly thirty years as a pastor, professor, certified biblical counselor, and certified Christian conciliator and church-conflict interventionist and trainer.

My own interest in biblical peacemaking began in the mid-1980s when I graduated from Trinity Evangelical Divinity School and, at twenty-six, became the pastor of a small church in Hurricane, West Virginia. The church had suffered a severe split, and the congregation I joined was the bleeding remnant. The aftershocks of that conflict were real, and I knew little about handling them. In time I became increasingly hungry to know how to better shepherd my people, so I began attending the annual biblical counseling training week provided each June by the Christian Counseling and Educational Foundation (CCEF) in a northern suburb of Philadelphia. As my wife and church family would attest, that training changed my life and ministry radically.

The guest plenary speaker one summer was Ken Sande, president of Peacemaker Ministries, who presented an early version of his Peacemaker seminar materials. As a young pastor I was attracted to both Ken's wise, biblical content and his winsome, gracious manner. His teaching that week sparked a special interest that God has fanned for over two decades now. Along with my ongoing training in biblical counseling through CCEF, the National Association of Nouthetic Counselors, and Westminster Theological Seminary (DMin), I began to attend the annual conferences of Peacemaker Ministries. I soon entered their conciliator training program and was invited to serve on their church intervention teams. I continue to serve adjunctively with Peacemaker Ministries in various roles.

This book is based on a simple three-step model with a four-word memory hook: Step 1—Please God; Step 2—Repent; and Step 3—Love. In other words, focus on God, then me (and my part in the conflict), and then the other person. We begin with two introductory chapters. In chapter 1 we behold the "God of peace" and trace his peacemaking work through the book of Romans. There we meet him as the God who makes peace with us through the cross of Jesus, pours out his inner peace on us and into us, guarantees us future worldwide peace, and calls and enables us to pursue relational peace with everyone. Chapter 2 overviews a biblical way to look at conflicts from God's vantage point. Conflicts are inevitable and sinful, but they also provide rich opportunities for spiritual growth for us and others. With chapter 3 we begin walking down the three-step peacemaking path, starting with a commitment, in response to God's saving grace, to make pleasing him our life goal and our conscious pursuit amid conflict. In chapters 4–6 we unpack Step 2. We address what it means to humbly identify, repent of, and confess our sins—both our heart sins and our behavioral sins—before both God and others.

With chapter 7 we transition into Step 3—what loving the other person looks like—which covers the rest of the book. Chapter 7 summarizes key attitudes—relational graces—we need to adopt toward the other party. Chapters 8–9 explore forgiveness, starting with God's forgiveness of us and then our forgiveness of others in both the attitudinal (unconditional) and the transacted (repentance-based) levels of forgiveness. We give special attention to dealing with the problem of bitterness. In chapter 10 we address the loving but oft-neglected practice of rebuke, answering a half-dozen *when*, *how*, *why*, and *what-if* questions. The last two chapters look at the final and ongoing steps, depending on the other person's responses to our previous efforts. Chapter 11 focuses on how to strengthen a reconciled relationship, including principles of communication and joint decision making when you and the other person have a difference of opinion on an important matter. Chapter 12 gives counsel on how to relate—how to minister with God's grace—to someone who hardens himself and will not be reconciled.

Acknowledgments

It takes a community to write a book. Behind this one lies such a body of influencers. I am grateful to the Lord for using countless people to train, challenge, and encourage me in my own pursuit of peace, in my work of conciliating and training others, and in my writing this book.

I think today of my past and present church families. Before coming to Southeastern Baptist Theological Seminary I ministered for nineteen years as the lead pastor of Grace Fellowship Church, in Hurricane, West Virginia. The leaders generously provided me with the time and expenses to pursue thorough peacemaking training. They patiently bore with my early attempts to teach the truths embedded in this book and to train our members. And they freed me to serve on and lead church intervention teams. After this, when I moved to Raleigh to teach at Southeastern, the Lord led my family and me to another first-rate church, Open Door Baptist, where I am privileged to serve as an elder and to lead our counseling and conciliation ministries.

Peacemaker Ministries provided the bulk of my biblical peacemaking training through their annual conferences, their writings, and their practical, professional-grade certification program and advanced seminars. Nearly every chapter of this book reflects the insights of Ken Sande and my "PM network" of friends and mentors. Thank you, Ken, Gary Friesen, Dave Edling, Rick Friesen, Annette Friesen, Jerry Wall, Paul Cornwell, Corlette Sande, Glenn Waddell, Lynn Pace, Ted Kober, Tara Barthel, Alfred Poirier, Kris Hart, and others who have modeled peacemaking, taught and encouraged me, and invited me to serve with you in various ways. In fact, if you and CCEF were ever to marry, I would not know which side of the wedding aisle to sit on. Your influence spreads far wider than Billings, Montana.

I thank God for the hundreds of individuals, couples, and families who have invited me into their struggles with conflicts and allowed me to apply the gospel of our Redeemer-Peacemaker. To that list I could add two dozen churches, Christian schools, and denominations who have allowed me to teach peacemaking seminars to their congregations and staff or to provide church-wide conflict intervention and leader-level mediation.

I am grateful also for my students. For seven years I have taught these conflict-resolution materials in masters' and DMin classes as a full-time professor at Southeastern and as a visiting professor at other schools to men and women training for ministry. Their insights enlighten me, their questions stir me, and their enthusiasm for Christ-centered peacemaking propels me.

God has also blessed me and my Patterson Hall colleagues at Southeastern with a skilled pair of faculty secretaries, Billie Goodenough and Carrie Pickelsimer. Thank you, ladies, for reading each chapter, offering insightful comments, and helping me maintain my campus duties amid writing deadlines.

I am honored to partner with Crossway for this project, having appreciated for many years the Christ-centered emphases their publications champion. I'm especially grateful to Al Fisher for giving me this opportunity, to Jill Carter for her administrative guidance, and to Thom Notaro for his careful editing. Nothing humbles a writer more than receiving back his original manuscript and finding each page laced with suggested improvements. Thank you, Thom, for making this book much better than I deserve. (Except for his "sorry" pun early in chapter 6 and the split infinitives he kindly allowed, any other writing faults are mine.)

I am especially grateful for my wife, Lauren, and the twenty-nine years of marriage that our Lord has given to us. Thank you, Dearie, for showing me how to pursue peace and for creating a peaceful home. Even during our occasional marital clashes we have learned much about Jesus, ourselves, and each other, and I wouldn't trade away a day of the joy, peace, and pleasure we have experienced together in Jesus Christ.

Above all, I think today of my Savior God—Father, Son, and Holy Spirit—who has brought me the fullness of his multidimensional peace that chapter 1 summarizes. To that overview we now turn.

1

Finding Hope in the God of Peace

To all in Rome who are loved by God and called to be saints:
Grace and peace to you from God our Father and from the Lord Jesus Christ.
Romans 1:7

If it is possible, as far as it depends on you, live at peace with everyone.
Romans 12:18

Maybe you can relate to Jen and Rick. Jen had been a believer in Jesus all her life. When she married after high school, she had high hopes for a happy marriage. The first two years sailed by blissfully. She and Rick both proclaimed the joys of marriage. But an assortment of ongoing conflicts soon developed. *Should we have children, and when? How will we cover our expenses? What involvement should we have with our parents who seem so meddlesome, and why won't my spouse stand up to them?* Along with these questions Jen found herself increasingly upset over Rick's workaholism and his lack of involvement in her life. Rick concurrently grumbled about Jen's critical spirit toward him. His frustrations grew. He had become a follower of Jesus only a year before they married, and his dreams of a truly Christian marriage were fading fast. If this trend continued unchecked, Rick and Jen would soon become another divorce statistic.

Or maybe your conflict concerns your church. Having worked tirelessly in the children's ministry for six years, Joanie had serious questions about the changes made by Gail, the new children's director. Joanie tried to get to know her, to understand her, and to support her, but their brief conversations proved unfruitful. Gail's answers seemed evasive, and Joanie increasingly sensed that her questions irritated Gail. Yet in the back of her mind her discouragement mounted. *Doesn't Gail know that changing the Wednesday night program will disturb parents? Does she even care?* Worse, Joanie was not alone. Several of her co-teachers voiced similar concerns to Joanie and each other. And so Joanie wondered, *Maybe it's time for me to take a break from ministering to kids and to consider another ministry.*

We could multiply examples not only from the arenas of marriage and church but also involving parents and children, roommates, and the workplace. Surely we and the many conflicted people around us need help with peacemaking.

But why a book on *biblical* peacemaking? Does the Bible really have something crucial to contribute to the real world of marriage fights, parent-teen breakdowns, job tensions, and church splits?

Yes, for two reasons. First, peace and conflict are Scripture megathemes. The Bible is all about God and his peace-pursuing, peacemaking activities. Its story line from Genesis through Revelation records conflict—earthly and cosmic, natural and supernatural. The paradise of Genesis 1–2 disintegrates swiftly into the disaster of Genesis 3. There, as the Scripture's curtain lifts, we see the war between God and Satan, and between God's people and Satan's people. Chapter after chapter in the Bible records victories and losses. The casualties are great; souls lie strewn across the Bible's battlefield. The combat continues through human history—raging throughout Israel's history, heightening at the Prince of Peace's birth, intensifying at his cross and resurrection, and culminating in Revelation 20's last battle, where we witness the final revolt, overthrow, and destruction of the Devil and all who belong to him. After that—but not one hour before—will the Peacemaker's work be finally done, as fractured humanity enjoys flawless harmony. In short, the Scriptures breathe conflict out of every pore. Between the Bible's two bookend chapters—prewar peace in Genesis 1–2 and post-war peace in Revelation 21–22—lie nearly twelve hundred chapters of hostility, aggression, alienation, and betrayal. You cannot read your Bible well and miss its militant plot; it is the ultimate "war and peace" novel. We long for the eternal day when, as theologians and hymn writers put it, the church militant will become the church triumphant.

The second reason to view your Bible as indispensable for peacemaking is that Scripture is all about our relationships—with God *and* with others. Are you ever tempted to think that the essence of Christian living is vertical only? *What really matters is praying unceasingly and communing continually with Jesus. If I can also have peaceful relationships, that would be nice too.* But having God-pleasing relationships is not a dispensable luxury. It is more than icing on a good Christian's cake. It lies at the heart of Christian discipleship. In his two great commandments, Jesus inseparably linked loving God with loving our neighbor, teaching us that the second is like the first and that the two together summarize all the Law and the Prophets (Matt. 22:37–40). You simply cannot love God without loving your neighbor. The apostle John elaborates, "If anyone says, 'I love God,' yet hates his brother, he is a liar. For anyone who does not love his brother, whom he has seen, cannot love God, whom he has not seen" (1 John 4:20). To devour your Bible, enjoy rich corporate worship, maintain personal purity, and tell dozens of people about Jesus—the sum of Christian living for some people—is simply not enough if your interpersonal relationships crumble.

For these reasons this book will help you handle your daily tensions with others. You have conflict in your life. You encounter it, admit it, and somehow endure it. You see it in your own home, in your place of work, and among your extended family. It flows through the water supply of your relational system. Conflict marks your parents, your children, your city, your coworkers, and even your church. (In fact, the odds are high that your church began out of conflict sometime long ago, as many do.) But you are not sure how to handle it, you too often contribute to it, and you sometimes mismanage it.

The Starting Place: Our Peacemaking God

So where do we begin? Like any subject, the proper starting place to think biblically about pursuing peace is God. And here is the central truth about God we need to start with: our God is the God of peace, his Son is the Prince of Peace, and his Spirit brings peace. And what has this God done? He has made peace with us, he pours out his peace on us and into us, and he calls and enables us to pursue peace with others.

The Bible links peace and God in at least four ways: There is the *saving peace* that God made with us at the cross, and the ongoing *inner peace* God gives us in our souls. These twin gifts in turn bring two more blessings for the Christian believer. They enable us to pursue *relational peace* with others in this life. Moreover, they guarantee us an endless life of future *situational peace* in the world to come, "a new heaven and a new earth, the home of righteousness" (2 Pet. 3:13).

From many authors in many passages, these four divine-peace provisions weave their way through the Scriptures. Let's think about these promises in light of the whole Bible and along the way envision the help they give to Joanie, Rick, and Jen.

We will start with Paul's first letter in the New Testament canon, the epistle to the Romans. Hailed by countless scholars as the greatest gospel treatise ever penned, it brilliantly describes and declares the peacemaking work of God. The reason is obvious: the gospel of Jesus is the gospel of peace.

Saving Peace with God

We learn from the opening verses of Romans that this letter is all about the gospel of God, which centers in his Son. It is the good news of God's saving grace in Jesus for sinners like me and you. And that good news is all about God's peace. Paul closes his introduction with this promise and blessing: "To all in Rome who are loved by God and called to be saints: Grace and peace to you from God our Father and from the Lord Jesus Christ" (Rom. 1:7).

These words come to us as more than mere formalities. They declare life-giving hope to seize and believe. The apostle announces God's stance—his posture of grace and peace toward us in Christ. Just as the words "loved" and "saints" point back to the designation of God's people in the Hebrew Scriptures,[1] so this promise of peace calls to mind the great Hebrew word *shalom* and the Old Testament vision of peace, fulfilled in Romans in the person and work of Jesus. It is no wonder that the formal worship liturgy in some Reformed churches frequently begins with an opening salutation, a word of greeting from God through the minister, often taken from texts like Romans 1:7.

Probably the most famous *shalom* prayer-promise comes from Numbers 6:24–26, the benediction assigned for Aaron and his sons to proclaim to God's people.

---

[1]Douglas J. Moo, *The Epistle to the Romans*, The New International Commentary on the New Testament (Grand Rapids: Eerdmans, 1996), 54.

> The LORD bless you
>   and keep you;
> the LORD make his face shine upon you
>   and be gracious to you;
> the LORD turn his face toward you
>   and give you peace.

This peace is more than the absence of war and strife. It is the positive presence of harmony, salvation, joy, blessing, and reconciliation—"the state of perfect well-being created by God's eschatological intervention and enjoyed by the righteous."[2] In the context of Romans, it is the reconciliation of believing Jews and believing Gentiles both with God and with each other—both vertical and horizontal. We taste it now whenever we enjoy the fruits of repentance, confession, and forgiveness with each other. One day we will experience it fully.

Who will experience this final peace? Only those who belong to God. The apostle both promises and warns, "There will be trouble and distress for every human being who does evil: first for the Jew, then for the Gentile; but glory, honor, and peace for everyone who does good: first for the Jew, then for the Gentile. For God does not show favoritism" (Rom. 2:9–11). Whether Jew or Gentile, the one who knows and follows the Redeemer God will treasure God's saving gift of *shalom*. On the other hand, the unbeliever who rejects God's "way of peace" (Rom. 3:17) will only reap God's judgment.

How does someone gain God's peace? Romans 5:1–2 replies, "Therefore, since we have been justified through faith, we have peace with God through our Lord Jesus Christ, through whom we have gained access by faith into this grace in which we now stand. And we rejoice in the hope of the glory of God." In this compact summary of gospel blessing, Paul tells us (1) that we now have peace with God; (2) that this peace is built on our justification through faith, God's grace-work of declaring us righteous in Christ; and (3) that this peace produces deep joy. As hymn writer Francis J. Van Alstyne (1820–1915) exclaimed,

> The vilest offender who truly believes,
>   that moment from Jesus a pardon receives.

---

[2]Ibid., 139. The term "eschatological" refers to God's final saving work at the end of time, which we begin to enjoy now.

Similar themes emerge in Ephesians 2:11–18, where Christ and his cross form the centerpiece of our peace.

What does this gospel assurance have to do with pursuing peace in our *relationships*? Everything. It fills us with joy, power, and confidence as we gratefully obey God in our relationships. It provides a model of grace to convey to others. And it reassures us that, even if the other people don't respond in kind, our relationship with the most important and ultimate Person in the universe remains secure. Thanks be to God for Jesus our Lord!

The saving work of God in the Christian, however, does not merely consist of a right standing with God. In salvation God has done something not only for us, but also *in* us. Our Christian growth—sanctification in its past, present, and future aspects—began with a decisive act by God of severing the spinal cord of sin and making us new people who are now inclined to love and obey him. The apostle Paul describes this internal transformation: "The mind of sinful man is death, but the mind controlled by the Spirit is life and peace; the sinful mind is hostile to God. It does not submit to God's law, nor can it do so. Those controlled by the sinful nature cannot please God" (Rom. 8:6–8). The sinful mind is hostile to God, but the saved mind—the mind captured and controlled by the Holy Spirit—reflects the very life and peace of God's Spirit, albeit imperfectly.

Isaiah pictures a similar reality with a vivid metaphor in Isaiah 57:18–21 concerning God's own promise to restore his people.

> "I have seen his ways, but I will heal him;
> I will guide him and restore comfort to him,
>   creating praise on the lips of the mourners in Israel.
> Peace, peace, to those far and near,"
>   says the LORD.[3] "And I will heal them."
> But the wicked are like the tossing sea,
>   which cannot rest,
>   whose waves cast up mire and mud.
> "There is no peace," says my God, "for the wicked."

[3]The apostle Paul also cites these words in Eph. 2:17, in the context of God's peacemaking work between Jews and Gentiles (Eph. 2:11–18) in the cross of Jesus. While I choose to walk through Romans, we could have profitably traced our theme through other epistles such as Ephesians or Philippians.

In other words—to join Isaiah and Paul—death marks the unbeliever; life and peace mark the believer.

Relational Peace with Others

The twin gifts of God's reconciling peace through Christ's cross and God's inner peace through his Spirit lead to the third peace blessing, namely, relational peace with others. In one of the Bible's most realistic texts concerning human relationships, Romans 12:18 exhorts us, "If it is possible, as far as it depends on you, live at peace with everyone." In many ways, our entire book will address these themes.

We find a fourfold call in this passage and its context. First, we must pursue peace as our Christian duty. The apostle commands us to live at peace. To fail to seek peace with people is to disobey God. We have no option.

Second, we must pursue peace with everyone. The peacemaking charge in this text is comprehensive; we must address all of our relationships. Our Lord does not permit us to ignore even one relationship or dismiss any individual. As the apostle declares in Acts 24:16, "So I strive always to keep my conscience clear before God and man." While this "with everyone" standard is admittedly high, God's power makes his commands less daunting.

Third, as we actively pursue peace, the apostle urges us to leave the results to God. "If it is possible," Paul reminds us, we should live at peace. He acknowledges that a peaceful result may not be possible; we have no guarantee that the other person will follow God's peacemaking plan. As the old saying goes, "It takes two to tango."

Fourth, keeping in mind the larger context, we must pursue peace in light of God's mercy toward us in Christ. The entire twelfth chapter of Romans flows from God's saving grace expounded in detail in Romans 1–11. "Therefore, I urge you, brothers, in view of God's mercy, to offer your bodies as living sacrifices, holy and pleasing to God—this is your spiritual act of worship" (12:1). In other words, we must apply Romans 12:18 against the backdrop of 12:1–2 and the preceding eleven chapters. Peacemaking is but one way we offer ourselves to God in sacrificial worship, and that obedience, like every other command in Romans 12, arises from the gospel of God's mercy in Christ.

With whom must we seek peace? While the context of Romans 12:18 primarily concerns pursuing peace with non-Christians, chapters 14–15 address our relationships with each other in the body of Christ. In the middle of his discussion he tells us what God treasures above all in his church: "For the kingdom of God is not a matter of eating and drinking, but of righteousness, peace and joy in the Holy Spirit, because anyone who serves Christ in this way is pleasing to God and approved by men" (Rom. 14:17–18). Five observations about the peace that Jesus prizes flow from this passage:

1. Peace, in this context, concerns our relationships with one another, that is, horizontal peace with each other more than vertical peace with God.
2. This peace is linked with "righteousness" and "joy" as central to God's kingdom.
3. Christ values these virtues over a person's individual convictions related to disputed areas of conduct like "eating" (kosher versus non-kosher food) or "drinking" (wine perhaps associated with idolatrous rituals).
4. This peace comes to us through the work of God's Holy Spirit (as seen in 15:13 below).
5. This peace concerns our relationships with one another (horizontal peace), and it pleases both God and other people.

Paul then inserts a summary challenge: "Let us therefore make every effort to do what leads to peace and to mutual edification" (14:19). "Make every effort" translates a Greek word elsewhere used for pursuing, tracking down, or persecuting someone or something. Like a hunter relentlessly hounding his prey, we must pursue peace with both Christians and non-Christians.

Thankfully, God has not left us alone in pursuing relational peace; he promises to be with us. The apostle rounds out the larger unit with a hope-giving wish prayer in Romans 15:13: "May the God of hope fill you with all joy and peace as you trust in him, so that you may overflow with hope by the power of the Holy Spirit." The joy and peace the gospel promises come to us solely as God's gifts. They come to us from God himself, the triune God of hope and peace. They come to us through the Holy Spirit's power, since "the fruit of the Spirit is love, joy, peace, patience," and so forth (Gal. 5:22–23). While this text could refer to inner peace (below), it likely refers to relational peace between members of the body.[4]

How do we actually receive these gifts? Do they somehow drop down from heaven or automatically pop up inside us? No. Romans 15:13 says that you receive these gifts "as you trust in God." While the cooperative working between God and the believer is a delicate subject, we must not overlook the fact that these blessings do not come to us apart from our faith. Only as we trust God will we experience his joy, peace, and hope in our relationships. By faith we can know these gifts in increasing measure. And as we practice biblical peacemaking—as we "make every effort to keep the unity of the Spirit through the bond of peace" (Eph. 4:3)—we will experience the Holy Spirit's help.

Inner Peace Enjoyed with the God of Peace

Our next two peace texts in Romans fasten our eyes on God himself by calling him "the God of peace" (15:33; 16:20; see also 1 Cor. 14:33; 2 Cor. 13:11; 1 Thess. 5:23; Heb. 13:20–21). In Romans 15:33, Paul again brings a wish prayer for God's people, a glorious benediction flowing from God's grace: "The God of peace be with you all. Amen." While the context does not specify the kind of peace Paul has in mind, his similar reference to the Lord as the "God of peace" in Philippians 4—a passage of promised blessing—suggests a reference to an inner peace of mind.

> Do not be anxious about anything, but in everything, by prayer and petition, with thanksgiving, present your requests to God. And the peace of God, which transcends all understanding, will guard your hearts and your minds in Christ Jesus. . . . Whatever you have learned or received or heard from me, or seen in me—put it into practice. And the God of peace will be with you. (Phil. 4:6–7, 9)

Paul first refers to the "peace of God"—the internal peace that God gives, in contrast to anxiety, as we pray and follow the apostle's life and teaching. Then he ends the section by designating this God as "the God of peace" who will be with us. If God himself is filled with peace (and he is), and if we are connected to him by faith (and we are), then we

---

[4]Moo, *Epistle to the Romans*, 881.

can and will experience this inner peace—his peace—in all its fullness. Here Paul echoes the promise of our Lord Jesus, "Peace I leave with you; my peace I give you. I do not give to you as the world gives. Do not let your hearts be troubled and do not be afraid" (John 14:27). As J. I. Packer puts it, "There is no peace like the peace of those whose minds are possessed with full assurance that they have known God, and God has known them, and that this relationship guarantees God's favour to them in life, through death, and on for ever."[5]

Future Global Peace Established by the God of Peace

Lastly, as the God of peace, he promises one more mighty *shalom* blessing: "The God of peace will soon crush Satan under your feet" (Rom. 16:20). Here the apostle Paul spans salvation history—from start to finish—in a single verse. He alludes to Genesis 3:15 and God's first redemptive promise to bring forth the "seed of the woman" (a reference to the Messiah) to destroy Satan. And who, says Paul, is the God who will act to fulfill salvation history? Paul explicitly calls him the "God of peace." In other words, it is God both as Redeemer and as *Peacemaker* who sent his Son to complete his saving program, destroy the Devil, and end the warfare begun in Genesis 3. In his return the Lord Jesus will bring about the final situational peace of paradise restored on earth. All our conflicts will be over forever, and books like the one you are reading will be unnecessary. "Amen. Come, Lord Jesus" (Rev. 22:20).

God: Our Hope for Peacemaking

Until then, what is our hope? God. Our God is the God of peace. He has made saving peace with us through Jesus Christ, he pours out his inner peace on us and into us, he promises future global peace, and he calls and enables us to pursue relational peace with others. There is not a person on the planet—including your spouse, child, parents, or business partner—with whom you cannot pursue peace. Herein, then, we find our own identity as we walk in the ways of God our Father. "Blessed are the peacemakers," said Jesus, "for they will be called sons of God" (Matt. 5:9). As we pursue peace in all our

---

[5] J. I. Packer, *Knowing God* (Downers Grove, IL: InterVarsity, 1973), 26.

relationships and help others do the same, we reflect the character of our peacemaking God.

What does this look like for Jen, Rick, and Joanie? In Jesus and the power of his Spirit each one of them can find help and hope in this fourfold perspective: First, amid their conflicts with others, God has already acted to bring them peace with himself. However much they have failed, God has accepted them, forgiven them, adopted them, and declared them righteous in Christ. However many people may be against them, God is for them. Second, God has given them in his Word all the wisdom they need to know what to do, and God has given them in his Spirit all the power they need to do it. The rest of this book will unpack that wisdom, but humming in the background is the promise of God's enabling Spirit. Third, God promises by that same Spirit to grant each of them inner peace, the assurance that he is with them as they trust in him. Fourth, all their peace pursuing in their daily relationships is but a precursor to the final global peace that God will one day bring about, in his timing. Their current conflicts will all be resolved.

Conclusion

As we pursue what God says in his Word through the ensuing chapters, let's hear and believe, by faith, God's special promise of blessing. This is my prayer as we journey forward together through this book:

> May the God of peace, who through the blood of the eternal covenant brought back from the dead our Lord Jesus, that great Shepherd of the sheep, equip you with everything good for doing his will, and may he work in us what is pleasing to him, through Jesus Christ, to whom be glory for ever and ever. Amen. (Heb. 13:20–21)

FOR PERSONAL REFLECTION OR GROUP DISCUSSION

1. How should recognizing our previous hostile state against God and our present reconciled state with God change the way we as Christians relate each day to people around us? How does the gospel of Jesus Christ affect our relationships with others, especially amid conflicts?

2. Recall God's four peace provisions/promises in this chapter:

a. God made relational peace between him and us at the cross of Jesus.
b. God enables us to pursue relational peace with others.
c. God gives us his inner peace within our hearts.
d. God guarantees future, global situational peace when Jesus returns.

How might each of these four truths help you with a conflict you face now?

3. Write a prayer to God in which you acknowledge and thank God for the help and hope he provides in Christ, and in which you commit yourself afresh to following his ways to pursue peace.

2

A God's-Eye View of Conflict

The Bible teaches that we should see conflict neither as an
inconvenience nor as an occasion to force our will on others,
but rather as an opportunity to demonstrate the love
and power of God in our lives.
Ken Sande

Therefore, if you are offering your gift at the altar
and there remember that your brother has something against you,
leave your gift. . . . First go and be reconciled to your brother;
then come and offer your gift.
Jesus in Matthew 5:23–24

My first driver's license proved more valuable than I expected. It carried me through high school in New Jersey, college in New York, my first two years of seminary in Illinois, and then my honeymoon year of marriage in Iowa, where I served as a full-time intern pastor. But when I returned to Illinois for my final year of seminary as a married man with a new permanent residence, I was overdue for a new license. So I went to the Illinois DMV office. That's when I faced the dreaded test. The written exam? No, I aced that. The road test? Not required. The test I dreaded was the eye test.

Apparently I had made it all the way to my twenty-fourth year of life with no vision restrictions. But the Lake County examiner failed me that day. I needed glasses. So off to Sears Optical I went.

I will never forget that day. I entered a new world. I saw things along Chicago's North Shore I had never seen before. And even in the things I had seen before, I now saw details I had never noticed. Billboard fine print emerged. Colors brightened. Faces sharpened—including those of any angry motorists I frustrated with my scenery gawking.

While nothing in the terrain actually changed, my ability to see it did. To see things as they really were required corrective lenses. My distorted view of reality required radical remediation. And with clearer vision I could now gain helpful information from those billboards and not miss turns just because I could not read street signs.

My story—not unusual among first-time eyeglass wearers—illustrates an age-old truth: how you view something will allow you to diagnose it properly and treat it wisely. If I believe my sluggish body suffers from vitamin deficiency, I will consume vitamins. If I believe my sluggish car needs new spark plugs, I will get a tune-up. Diagnosis dictates treatment. Perception prescribes response.

What do you see when you look at conflict? What comes to your mind when you hear that word? Fighting? Anger? Avoidance? Division? Marriage? What attitudes do you hear others voice?

- "It's OK; that's just the way life is."
- "Conflict is normal, natural, and neutral."
- "I have my rights. Nobody's gonna step on me. I'm no doormat."
- "There's no way I can handle this. It's never gonna change."
- "I don't get mad; I get even."
- "It'll all work out. Time will heal things."
- "Let it rest. We need to move forward."

But what does God see when he sees conflict? What does he want us to see? These questions expose our vision problem. In our fallenness we don't see conflict the way God wants us to see it. That's where our journey must start.

If we put on biblical glasses to look at conflict, what will we see? Three hope-giving perspectives come into focus.

1. Realize that Conflicts Are Inevitable; Therefore Expect Them

Are you surprised that you face relational tensions? Don't be. In this life, count on conflicts. Why? Because we are fallen sinners living with fallen sinners in a fallen world. And one of the things that sinners do—a point less often admitted than we might think—is sin, and often against each other. In other words, we are sinners not only doctrinally but practically. The Bible of course assumes this, reminding us of this bleak reality from cover to cover:

- "There is not a righteous man on earth who does what is right and never sins" (Eccles. 7:20).
- "We all, like sheep, have gone astray, each of us has turned to his own way" (Isa. 53:6).
- "We have already made the charge that Jews and Gentiles alike are all under sin . . . , for all have sinned and fall short of the glory of God" (Rom. 3:9, 23).
- "If we claim to be without sin, we deceive ourselves and the truth is not in us. . . . If we claim we have not sinned, we make him out to be a liar and his word has no place in our lives" (1 John 1:8, 10).

We see the presence of conflict in every arena of life. Consider our marriage relationships. Genesis 1–2 pictures a perfect marriage, a marriage unlike any other, hand-fashioned by God himself. At the culmination of God's creation of humanity as male and female, God saw that his work was "very good" (Gen. 1:31). The next chapter of Genesis details Adam and Eve's conflict-free marriage.

Then the LORD God made a woman from the rib he had taken out of the man, and he brought her to the man.
The man said,

> "This is now bone of my bones
>   and flesh of my flesh;
> she shall be called 'woman,'
>   for she was taken out of man."

For this reason a man will leave his father and mother and be united to his wife, and they will become one flesh.
The man and his wife were both naked, and they felt no shame. (Gen. 2:22–25)

Indeed, if any marriage could warrant the descriptor "a marriage made in heaven," this one would! Everything about it, says God, was very good.

But turn one page and everything falls apart. Tragic problems erupt. Sin enters and alienation results (Gen. 3:1–7). The first and primary alienation is vertical: Adam and Eve's sin disrupts their communion with God (Gen. 3:8–11). But on the heels of this vertical falling out we find the seeds of horizontal alienation: the starting point for a breach between the husband and wife that would only increase through subsequent generations: "The man said, 'The woman you put here with me—she gave me some fruit from the tree, and I ate it'" (Gen. 3:12). God confronts Adam; Adam criticizes God and blames Eve.

The vertical and horizontal, of course, are inseparably related, as interconnected as Jesus's two great commandments to love God and love our neighbor (Matt. 22:37–40). The apostle John powerfully merges the two: "If anyone says, 'I love God,' yet hates his brother, he is a liar. For anyone who does not love his brother, whom he has seen, cannot love God, whom he has not seen. And he has given us this command: Whoever loves God must also love his brother" (1 John 4:20–21). The rest of the Bible, from Genesis through Revelation, records sin's ugly impact on both our vertical and horizontal relationships.

But along with our human disharmony, the Bible displays the Redeemer's plan of reconciliation that leads to a glorious restoration of all our relationships. As the Lord God forewarned the serpent,

> And I will put enmity
>> between you and the woman,
>> and between your offspring and hers;
> he will crush your head,
>> and you will strike his heel. (Gen. 3:15; also Gal. 4:4)

The offspring of the woman, Jesus Christ, would repair the breach, reverse the curse, and reconcile his people both to God and to each other. As Genesis teaches—its mega-theme—God demonstrates his unswerving commitment to bless his people despite every obstacle that threatens that blessing.

One benefit of grasping conflict's inevitability is to encourage us to persevere whenever conflict tempts us to give up on a relationship. Rick and Jen, mentioned in the previous chapter, came to the place in their conflicted marriage where they wondered whether they should have married in the first place. Can you imagine Adam and Eve, upon their fall into sin, questioning whether they should have married: "Maybe this wasn't such a good idea; maybe we made a mistake"? We laugh at that thought, but for many couples the eruption of conflict leads them to question the very foundation of their marriage choice. Of course, it's entirely possible that a couple married unwisely, but the presence of conflict, even severe conflict, does not prove it. The fact that sin marked even the first, God-fashioned marriage ought to encourage every married couple who has ever had a fight.

Why is marital conflict inevitable? Because sin remains in each spouse. The nineteenth-century British bishop J. C. Ryle understood the need for couples to grasp this reality. One of his "rules" for a couple to have a happy marriage is "not to expect too much from their partners, and to remember that marriage is, after all, the union of two sinners, and not of two angels."[1] (For those of us married for more than a weekend, this should present no surprise.) Elisabeth Elliot makes the same point: "When sinful people live in the same world, and especially when they work in the same office or sleep in the same bed, they sin against each other. Troubles arise. Some of those troubles are very serious and not subject to easy solutions." The good news? She continues, "God knows all about them, and knew about them long before they happened. He made provision for them."[2]

We should also not be surprised when conflict marks a parent-child relationship. In an amazing by-the-way statement, Jesus addresses parents, "If you, then, though you are evil, know how to give good gifts to your children, how much more will your Father in heaven give good gifts to those who ask him!" (Matt. 7:11). Jesus doesn't even assert or argue the fact of parental sin; he simply assumes it in passing: you are evil! (Can you imagine an American presidential candidate making that truth a plank in his policy platform?) It is no wonder that the apostle Paul recognizes the potential for fathers to exasperate their children and exhorts them against it (Eph. 6:4).

Nor are our children innocent. King David understood his own inborn depravity.

> Surely I was sinful at birth,
>   sinful from the time my mother conceived me. (Ps. 51:5)

---

[1] J. C. Ryle, *Expository Thoughts on the Gospel of Mark* (1857; Carlisle, PA: Banner of Truth, 1985), 200.
[2] Elisabeth Elliot, *Trusting God in a Twisted World* (Old Tappan, NJ: Revell, 1989), 96.

And he is not alone. The writer of Proverbs puts it this way, "Folly is bound up in the heart of a child" (Prov. 22:15). What are the "terrible twos" (or the "terrifying threes") but the progressive unpacking of the sin already bound up within each child? Based on this perspective Jay Adams offers prudent counsel to parents.

> Parents certainly can take a lot of the unnecessary grief out of child raising when, as a matter of course (rather than becoming falsely shocked over the fact), they expect their children to do wrong things at home, at school, and in public. There is then no necessity to subject children to unusual and inappropriate discipline or to the excessive anger that sometimes grows out of embarrassment. Once parents are prepared to admit that the Biblical doctrine of original sin is true not only in theory, but is operative as well in the life of little Mary or Johnny, they can relax and deal with the problem appropriately (Biblically).[3]

Given the sinfulness of both parents and children, how can conflict in the home not be inevitable?

Yet even if conflict marks our homes, surely when we come to our church-family relationships—the redeemed people of God—we will find harmony, right? Sadly, even Christians face frequent conflict with one another. The Bible's repeated exhortations to pursue peace assume that even brothers and sisters in the body of Christ will offend each other. Listen to the commands of our Lord Jesus:

- "Therefore, if you are offering your gift at the altar and there remember that your brother has something against you, leave your gift there in front of the altar. First go and be reconciled to your brother; then come and offer your gift" (Matt. 5:23–24).
- "If your brother sins against you, go and show him his fault, just between the two of you. If he listens to you, you have won your brother over" (Matt. 18:15).
- "If your brother sins, rebuke him, and if he repents, forgive him. If he sins against you seven times in a day, and seven times comes back to you and says, 'I repent,' forgive him" (Luke 17:3b–4).

---

[3]Jay E. Adams, *Christian Living in the Home* (Nutley, NJ: Presbyterian and Reformed, 1972), 12.

Jesus reminds us to expect sinful conflict. We will have fights with each other. To deny it is to ignore God's perspective.

We could expand the above to talk about workplace disputes, school bullying, clashes with neighbors, or in-law fights. No relationship under God's sun is conflict-free.

2. Realize that Conflicts Are Sinful; Therefore Resolve Them!

Like many couples in our day, Jimmy and Beth came from homes marked by divorce. Despite professions of faith in Jesus by both sets of parents, neither of those marriages modeled how to resolve conflicts Christ's way. And Jimmy and Beth basically followed the habitual patterns they watched in their families of origin.[4] They saw their moms and dads fight but not reconcile. Jimmy responded to his family's conflict style by becoming a confronter. Like his parents, he raised his voice to make his points. Beth instead chose to stuff her feelings, say nothing, and pull away from her husband when issues arose. And so their fights were frequently marked by Jimmy attacking and Beth retreating.

What made Jimmy and Beth's dance doubly difficult was that they had come to accept this dynamic as normal—"just the way we are." They resigned themselves to conflict's inevitability. On the one hand, they failed to grasp that conflicts are sinful and must be addressed.[5] Conflicts displease God. They arise from self-centered hearts. They involve hurtful words and actions. They alienate and separate people. They violate biblical teaching about love, unity, harmony, anger, and bitterness. They produce distance, disunity, and disharmony. Beth and Jimmy were complacently tolerating what grieved God! On the other hand, they also failed to grasp that their conflicts were resolvable and that God was committed to helping us handle such problems. In other words, they saw the inevitability but not the resolvability of conflict.

---

[4]I am not implying that Jimmy and Beth bore no responsibility (they did) or that parental sins *cause* children to imitate behaviors and attitudes (they don't). But I am observing the power that examples and influences can exert apart from godly commitments to have our minds transformed by God's truth and to unlearn ungodly patterns.

[5]While it is possible to speak of conflict in broader terms, e.g., uses in business-management theory or the biological sciences, both in the Bible and for the person on the street the term connotes something bad or sinful.

How should we respond to conflict? God calls us to resolve our conflicts actively, diligently, and immediately. We must deal with conflict actively, not assuming it will resolve itself. We must deal with it diligently, making concentrated, strenuous efforts to reconcile our relationships. And we must deal with it immediately, not delaying, postponing, or procrastinating.

Our Lord Jesus sets this active-diligent-immediate agenda with two complementary commands. In Matthew 5:23–25 he urges us, "Therefore, if you are offering your gift at the altar and there remember that your brother has something against you, leave your gift there in front of the altar. First go and be reconciled to your brother; then come and offer your gift. Settle matters quickly with your adversary." The aggressiveness of this agenda underscores Jesus's priorities about peacemaking. Then in Matthew 18:15–16 Jesus directs us, "If your brother sins against you, go and show him his fault, just between the two of you. If he listens to you, you have won your brother over. But if he will not listen, take one or two others along, so that 'every matter may be established by the testimony of two or three witnesses.'"

These passages, viewed together, form a powerful dynamic—what I call the "Matthew 5 and 18 Dynamic": When we have offended someone, *we* should go (Matt. 5:23–26); when someone has offended us, *we* also should go (Matt. 18:15–16). In either case, Jesus calls us to take the first step toward pursuing peace with others.

Christ's apostles echoed the same need for active-diligent-immediate effort. Note the urgency and energy required in their commands:

- "So I strive always to keep my conscience clear before God and man" (Acts 24:16).
- "If it is possible, as far as it depends on you, live at peace with everyone" (Rom. 12:18).
- "Let us therefore make every effort to do what leads to peace and to mutual edification" (Rom. 14:19).
- "Make every effort to keep the unity of the Spirit through the bond of peace" (Eph. 4:3).
- "Flee the evil desires of youth, and pursue righteousness, faith, love and peace, along with those who call on the Lord out of a pure heart" (2 Tim. 2:22).

- "Make every effort to live in peace with all men and to be holy; without holiness no one will see the Lord" (Heb. 12:14).

The cumulative effect of these half-dozen verses leaves no room for complacency or passivity. Instead, they constrain sincere Christians to cry out for the Holy Spirit's help in this formidable task.

These passages also mean, contrary to popular myth, that time does *not* heal all wounds. Conflicts will not mend themselves. People do not "get over" insults and injuries. Instead, unresolved conflicts scab over. They go underground, surfacing later, and sometimes with greater fury, animosity, or coldness. That's why relational reconciliation requires hard work. The above verses call us to "pursue" peace—to go after it, track it down, and hunt for it. Peacemaking is not easy or optional.

The good news for Beth and Jimmy was that they could unlearn their parents' wrong styles of conflict resolution. Thankfully, because of Christ their Redeemer, they were not doomed to repeat "the empty way of life handed down to you from your forefathers" (1 Pet. 1:18). Of course, old habits die slowly. It took some time for Beth and Jimmy to reorient their thinking. A turning point came in a counseling session when they realized how serious and ingrained their patterns were: "We've bickered and picked at each other for years now, not realizing how wrong it was and unaware that things could ever change." They resolved to no longer tolerate their constant fighting and with the help of God's Word, God's Spirit, and God's church—their pastor and their small group—they began to learn new, God-honoring ways to handle their problems.

3. Realize that Conflicts Are Opportunities;[6] Therefore Seize Them

"Conflicts are *what*?" you ask. "*Opportunities*? What planet did you come from?"

I understand your response. We all recoil against the word *conflict* and wish it did not invade our lives. But thankfully the inevitability and sinfulness of conflict are not God's last words. Part of the hope of the

---

[6]See also Ken Sande, *The Peacemaker: A Biblical Guide to Resolving Personal Conflict*, 3rd ed. (Grand Rapids: Baker, 2004), 31–41. I am indebted to Sande for his helpful insights on this entire third perspective and throughout the following pages.

gospel is that God redeems not only our lives but also our situations. He aims to use every hardship we face, including interpersonal conflict, for a good purpose. Romans 8:28–29 reminds us that our sovereign God uses "all things"—including in that Romans 8 context a host of hardships and suffering—to conform Christians into Jesus's likeness. Once we view relational conflict in the broader biblical category of "trials," then the world of biblical comfort and purpose opens up to us. In other words, conflict becomes an opportunity for God to advance his life-shaping agenda in our lives.

What are the opportunities for greater good that conflict provides?

1. Relational conflicts provide opportunities for us to know God better, draw near to him, and please him. The next chapter will focus on pleasing God as the foundational step in pursuing peace. Here we consider what we can learn about God if we seek him amid our conflicts. For one thing, we see God as our *forgiver*, the one who pardons both us and the other party for our respective contributions to the conflict.[7] In his classic book on Christ-centered community, *Life Together*, Dietrich Bonhoeffer insightfully observes the benefit we can derive from seeing the sins of others.

> Will not his sin be a constant occasion for me to give thanks that both of us may live in the forgiving love of God in Jesus Christ? Thus the very hour of disillusionment with my brother becomes incomparably salutary, because it so thoroughly teaches me that neither of us can ever live by our own words and deeds, but only by that one Word and Deed which really binds us together—the forgiveness of sins in Jesus Christ![8]

When I see my own sins exposed, or when I feel the irritation or anger of mistreatment by others leveled against me, I have an opportunity to see afresh the God who forgives sins.

We also come to see other aspects of our God. He is our *empowerer*, the one who helps us grow as Christians and enables us by his Holy Spirit to put off sin and put on righteousness. When faced with conflict, we may feel weak and helpless. At that point God offers himself to us as

---

[7]We will address God's forgiveness of us and our forgiveness of others in chap. 7.
[8]Dietrich Bonhoeffer, *Life Together: The Classic Exploration of Faith in Community*, trans. John W. Doberstein (New York: HarperCollins, 1954), 28.

> our refuge and strength,
>> an ever-present help in trouble. (Ps. 46:1)

Further, God rises up as our *protector*, the one who comforts and assures us when others attack or mistreat us. Moreover, he towers over us as our *judge*, the one who will hold us accountable for our conduct amid conflict (and thereby humble us in our relationships with others), and the one who will one day vindicate us and reverse all unjust accusations against us.

2. Relational conflicts give us opportunities to become more like Jesus. God uses interpersonal hardships as the testing ground and springboard for our spiritual maturation. In what ways? Let me suggest seven specific ways that God might use conflict to transform you into his likeness.

1. God might use this conflict to *enhance* and deepen our relationship with him. In times of conflict Christians tend to pray more, read their Bible more, and think about God more.

> Before I was afflicted I went astray,
>> but now I obey your word. (Ps. 119:67)

Conflicts can deepen our dependence on the Lord.

2. God might use this conflict to allow us to *experience* the sufferings of Jesus. In times of conflict we taste—albeit in a lesser way—something of his rejection and mistreatment. "I want to know Christ and the power of his resurrection and the fellowship of sharing in his sufferings" (Phil. 3:10). Conflicts can connect us more intensely to our suffering Savior.

3. God might use this conflict to *expose* our remaining sin. In times of conflict God's Spirit surfaces our sins and leads us to repentance, faith, and godly change. "Remember how the LORD your God led you all the way in the desert these forty years, to humble you and to test you in order to know what was in your heart, whether or not you would keep his commands" (Deut. 8:2). Conflicts can show us the real us, with all our ugly flaws, and give us renewed opportunities to grow in Christlikeness.

4. God might use this conflict to *exhibit* to others his work in us. In times of conflict we demonstrate to onlookers our love and trust in Jesus. As Jesus taught his disciples in the context of conflict and persecution,[9] "You are the light of the world. . . . In the same way, let your light shine before men, that they may see your good deeds and praise your Father in heaven" (Matt. 5:14–16). Conflicts can give us the opportunity to spotlight God and his Son.

5. God might use this conflict to *engage* us more actively in the body of Christ. In times of conflict we can draw near to fellow church members who can support us, pray for us, weep with us, coach us, and challenge us to handle the conflict in a God-pleasing way. "Rejoice with those who rejoice; mourn with those who mourn" (Rom. 12:15). Conflicts can link us more intentionally and visibly to our church family.

6. God might use this conflict to *equip* us to minister to others with greater wisdom, sensitivity, and empathy. In times of conflict God helps us not only for our good but also so that we can help others. "Praise be to the God and Father of our Lord Jesus Christ, the Father of compassion and the God of all comfort, who comforts us in all our troubles, so that we can comfort those in any trouble with the comfort we ourselves have received from God" (2 Cor. 1:3–4). Conflicts can prepare us to more effectively help others handle their conflicts.

7. God might use this conflict to *elevate* our desire for Christ's return and the new heaven and earth, where peace prevails and righteousness reigns. In times of conflict, we feel properly dissatisfied with this fallen world, and we long for the next. "Therefore, prepare your minds for action; be self-controlled; set your hope fully on the grace to be given you when Jesus Christ is revealed" (1 Pet. 1:13). Conflicts can whet our appetite for Jesus to come back.

How then should we look at something that has the potential to (1) deepen our dependence on the Lord, (2) connect us more intensely to him, (3) show us our sin so we can grow more in Christ, (4) allow us to spotlight God and his Son, (5) link us more intentionally and visibly to the church, (6) prepare us for more effective service, and (7) help

---

[9]While there may be some implications for evangelical social or political action in this image of Christians as light of the world, the context concerns how we conduct ourselves in relation to others when facing opposition.

us long for Christ's return? The word *opportunity* richly summarizes these dynamics.

Of course, all this assumes that we desire Christlikeness more than immediate comfort, and we treasure our Christian growth above situational relief. If we are honest, we must admit that too often our desire to be like Jesus falls short at this point, leading us to avoid conflict and not pursue peace. We crave circumstantial improvement more than the sanctifying opportunities that conflict affords. The cure involves remembering the depth of our sin, seeing afresh God's saving mercy, depending on the Spirit's help, and obeying the call to please God and to live for the Savior who died and rose for us.

3. Relational conflicts give us opportunities to love and minister to others—both those with whom we have conflict and those who are watching. In our last chapter we will examine Luke 6:27–36, in which Jesus calls us to love our enemies and show them mercy: "But I tell you who hear me: Love your enemies, do good to those who hate you, bless those who curse you, pray for those who mistreat you. . . . Be merciful, just as your Father is merciful" (vv. 27–28, 36). While we may label some individuals as enemies, most of our conflicted relationships don't descend to that level. The other party may be a parent, spouse, pastor, or coworker. Nevertheless, we may learn from our Lord's counsel how to treat graciously even friends and family members who are enemy-like in their conduct toward us. (We will address these hard cases in chap. 11.) In such cases Jesus calls us to love and serve the other person. "For even the Son of Man did not come to be served, but to serve, and to give his life as a ransom for many" (Mark 10:45).

What does this look like for Beth and Jimmy? Here's what I shared with them as one of their pastors: "Jimmy and Beth, I don't want to minimize the severity of your conflicts. They are serious. But let me encourage you that God was not and is not asleep, and you do not face them alone. He is a good God and he has an agenda to free you and transform you. As you seek to follow the Lord, with your pastors' help, your conflicts will become opportunities for you to get closer to him in new and fresh ways. You can know him as the one who forgives you and the one who comforts and strengthens you. In addition, he wants to use conflict, like any hardship, to make you more like Jesus and to mature you. He wants to make you more dependent on him and to teach you grace, love, wisdom, and compassion toward each other. And he wants to cultivate a new and growing marriage between you that will honor him. Let me urge you to follow his peacemaking path. . . ."

Conclusion

With our biblical glasses on, we can view our conflicts differently. Because they are inevitable, we can expect them and not be shocked when they come. Because they are sinful, we must commit to pursuing reconciliation—actively, diligently, and immediately. And because they are opportunities, we can seize them to our spiritual profit.

As Jimmy and Beth became conscious of their attack-retreat dynamics and how displeasing to God their conflicts were, they confessed them before God and each other. In turn, they seized each recurrence as an opportunity to experience afresh both God's pardoning and his empowering grace. They increasingly saw previously hidden pockets of judgmentalism and fear, and they became more effective in helping their friends deal with their conflicts. They have not arrived, but they are on the right road.

For Personal Reflection or Group Discussion

1. Which of the above three perspectives do you sometimes forget, and how can you better keep them in mind and apply them to the conflicts you face?

2. Think of a conflict that a friend or family member faces. Which of the above perspectives do you think he might not see clearly? How might you communicate that perspective to him? What might you say?

3. Spend some time reviewing the Scripture passages above, and ask God to give you a new vision of conflict. Journal some personal reflections on how these perspectives apply to a current conflict. Share these with a mature Christian friend or a church leader for added accountability and blessing.

3

Keeping God Central

Pleasing Him amid Conflict

No matter how large the crowds,
they danced for only one audience: Mr. B.
Jean Fleming, on the New York City Ballet Company's reverence
for longtime ballet master George Balanchine

May the words of my mouth and the meditation of my heart
be pleasing in your sight,
O Lᴏʀᴅ, my Rock and my Redeemer.
Psalm 19:14

In our first two chapters we laid several foundational blocks. We saw
that God has made peace with us through Jesus, that he fills us with his
peace, that he has destined us for a glorious place of peace, and that he
calls and enables us to pursue peace with others. Moreover, to pursue
peace with others, we need a threefold perspective: to expect conflicts
as inevitable in this fallen world; to seek to resolve conflicts because
they are sinful; and to seize conflicts as God-given opportunities to
know him better and grow in our faith. And our God assures us that
he, the God of peace, will help us.

That leads to the big question this book addresses: How exactly
should we pursue peace with others? What does it look like? What
steps should we take?

In this and the following chapters we will follow a simple three-
pronged process to pursue relational peace: (1) Please God, (2) Repent,

and (3) Love. Figure 1[1] summarizes our model. The triangle at the top represents the triune God who has revealed himself to us in Jesus Christ (the cross symbol). The thick arrow coming from God represents his initiating and all-sufficient grace, which he provides in countless ways. This arrow is thicker than the others since the initiative and power come from God. We could replace the summary term "grace" with verbs like *loves, serves, forgives,* and *listens,* depending on the specific relational graces the conflicted parties need. The parties might be a husband and wife (or any man or woman) as pictured, or two friends, or many more figures representing groups of people. (While the diagram highlights only one party's response, the other party should reciprocate the action.) The three thinner arrows represent the three-step response to God's grace: (1) Please God, (2) Repent, and (3) Love. We will unpack the first in this chapter and various aspects of the other two in the ensuing chapters.

Figure 1. Three-step model for resolving conflict

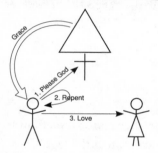

We begin by exploring a simple yet foundational truth and consider its many implications for Christ-centered conflict resolution: Our goal in life is to please God.[2]

What does it mean to please God? Simply put, to please God means to bring him delight by being and doing what he desires. In this sense, pleasing God is no different than pleasing anyone else: we find out what

---

[1] I used a similar diagram in my article, "God's Place in Your Marriage," *The Journal of Biblical Counseling* 17, no. 1 (Fall 1998): 44–46.

[2] While the Bible gives many synonymous ways to summarize what it means to relate rightly to God—"glorify" God, "love" God, "obey" God, "walk with" God—I have chosen "pleasing" God instead of "glorifying" God because for most people it seems less abstract, less "spiritual," and more practical, and because "pleasing" God appears more frequently in the New Testament (John 5:30; 8:28–29; Rom. 14:17–18; 2 Cor. 5:9; Eph. 5:8–10; Col. 1:10–12; 1 Thess. 4:1–2; 2 Tim. 2:3–4; Heb. 11:5–6; 13:20–21; 1 John 3:21–22).

the person wants us to be or do, and we seek to be or do that. We discern what delights the Lord—what brings him pleasure—and we follow that path, eliciting his smile and fulfilling his purpose in creating and redeeming us.

> **The Path for Pursuing Peace**
> **Step 1. Please God**
> Step 2. Repent
> Step 3. Love the person

In 2 Corinthians 5:1–8 the apostle ponders his imminent future. Will he suffer death from his persecutors and thereby go to be with the Lord, gaining the eternal, heavenly body God has guaranteed him, or will he continue to live on this earth, groaning in this mortal bodily "tent"? While he can't control these contingencies, and there are advantages to each, Paul's preference would be to leave his mortal body and be home with Jesus (vv. 6–8).

While both prospects are worthy options, in verse 9 Paul makes an amazing statement. There is something more important than either contingency. "So we make it our goal to please him, *whether* we are at home in the body *or* away from it." In other words, what is ultimately important is not *whether* he lives or dies but *how* he lives or dies—whether or not he pleases God. If Paul continues on this earth, then his goal is to please God. If death takes him to be with the Lord, then his goal is to please God. Whatever happens, Paul fixates on pleasing the Lord.

This mind-set of pleasing God whether A or B happens carries powerful applications to relationships. I must seek to please God *whether* my spouse treats me kindly *or* treats me poorly. I must seek to please God *whether* my boss promotes me *or* bypasses me. I must seek to please God *whether* my roommate is a neat-freak *or* a slob. Whatever eventuality I face or providence God permits, my goal is clear: I must make it my aim to please God.

Why must we seek to please God? Because God is watching. Verse 10 reminds us, "For we must all appear before the judgment seat of Christ, that each one may receive what is due him for the things done while in the body, whether good or bad." One day every believer will be judged by the Lord, not for condemnation (Rom. 8:1) but for rewards and for his commendation, "Well done."

Yet the proper fear of final judgment is not the only motive that drives the apostle and by no means the highest or most dominant. In fact, the rest of the Bible points to a higher motive for the son or daughter of God. The highest motive appears a few verses later: "For Christ's love compels us, because we are convinced that one died for all, and therefore all died. And he died for all, that those who live should no longer live for themselves but for him who died for them and was raised again" (2 Cor. 5:14–15).

While the call in verse 9 is to please God, the parallel call in verse 15 is to live for Jesus—to live for the Savior who died and rose for us. What will generate this selfless agenda? It is Jesus Christ's love for us. What does Christ's love do for Paul? It "compels" him. The Greek verb carries the idea of being constrained or pressured by something, the way squeezing a toothpaste tube propels the paste out of the tube. As one New Testament scholar observes, "The rendering that best captures this dual notion of constraint and restraint is 'controls (us).' Christ's love is a compulsive force in the life of believers, a dominating power that effectively eradicates choice in that it leaves them no option but to live for God (v. 13a) and Christ (v. 15b)."[3] Grasping God's compelling love drives us to live for him.

If Christ's love is so dominantly compelling, how does Paul know it? Did he stroll along a flowered hillside and hear in his mind soft organ music and a still small voice whispering, "I love you, I love you, I love you"? No. He tells us: "Because we are convinced. . . ." Paul's assurance that Jesus loves him arises from reasoned conviction based on firm facts: "We are convinced that one died for all." As he declares in Romans 5:8, "But God demonstrates his own love for us in this: While we were still sinners, Christ died for us."

Convinced of God's love rooted in Christ's death and resurrection for him, Paul summarizes the motivational rhythm of grace-centered living: I now live for him who died and rose for me. Jesus's cross and resurrection change me. By his Spirit Jesus converts me from living for myself to living for him. No life goal is more worthy for a Christian than to learn daily what it means to be a "died-for" and "raised-for" person. Jesus and his cross and resurrection must propel our peacemaking efforts.

Biblical Principles about Pleasing God

Before we explore how a commitment to please God transforms the way we handle conflicts, let me summarize five truths about pleasing God.

---

[3]Murray J. Harris, *The Second Epistle to the Corinthians: A Commentary on the Greek Text*, New International Greek Text Commentary (Grand Rapids: Eerdmans, 2005), 419.

1. We must make pleasing God our single, all-consuming life goal. In addition to 2 Corinthians 5:9 and 5:15 above, the apostle Paul pictures the centrality of pleasing God with a straightforward metaphor: "Endure hardship with us like a good soldier of Christ Jesus. No one serving as a soldier gets involved in civilian affairs—he wants to please his commanding officer" (2 Tim. 2:3–4). The soldier's aim is simple and singular: Obey your commanding officer. Do not distract yourself with civilian matters. Discern and do what pleases your CO.

Here is a life goal that is simple, clear, and uncomplicated. Not easy, but simple. Do you know the difference? My seminary students call me a tough professor who gives hard exams. I don't know if that's true, but I do know that it is quite simple to get an A on my exams: simply master the course lecture materials and assigned readings for the exam. It's simple—not complicated, not complex, not cluttered—but also not easy. There is a lot of material to study and review carefully. Earning an A on an exam requires hard work.

Is it easy to please God? No, it's hard; it requires self-denial and strong effort. But it is simple—clear and uncomplicated. Simply discern what delights God and do it. Aim your life at the Bible's bull's-eye of believing and obeying God's Word. Simple; not easy.

2. We must seek to please God, not ourselves or others. The Scriptures contrast pleasing God with pleasing yourself. If anyone on this earth ever had a right to please himself, it was the God-man, Jesus, but Paul tells us that "even Christ did not please himself" (Rom. 15:3). Jesus did not exercise a self-pleasing prerogative. Instead, he declares, "I seek not to please myself but him who sent me" (John 5:30). "I always do what pleases him" (John 8:29). We are never more like Jesus than when we aim entirely to please God.

The Bible also contrasts pleasing God with pleasing others in the appeasing, fear-of-people sense. Paul confronts the Galatians with a fundamental question: "Am I now trying to win the approval of men, or of God? Or am I trying to please men? If I were still trying to please men, I would not be a servant of Christ" (Gal. 1:10). He then demonstrates that Christ-centered boldness in the next chapter when he confronts his fellow apostle, Peter, for the sin of people pleasing (Gal. 2:11–13).

3. We must seek to please God according to God's Word. So far we have assumed that we know what pleases God. But *how* do we know? Listen to Paul's answer in 1 Thessalonians 4:1–2: "Finally, brothers, *we instructed you* how to live in order to please God, as in fact you are living. Now we ask you and urge you in the Lord Jesus to do this more and more. For you know *what instructions we gave you* by the authority of the Lord Jesus." Similarly, 1 John 3:22 connects the two: "We obey his commands and do what pleases him." We learn what pleases God from apostolic instruction—from our Bibles.

In terms of pursuing peace, relational peace is one explicit virtue commanded in God's Word: "For the kingdom of God is not a matter of eating and drinking, but of righteousness, peace and joy in the Holy Spirit, because anyone who serves Christ in this way is pleasing to God and approved by men" (Rom. 14:17–18). Peacemaking pleases God.

4. We must seek to please God by depending on God's power. As we observed above, while pleasing God is simple, it is not easy. We need powerful help to pull it off; nothing short of supernatural assistance will suffice. We need external power; we don't have the energy naturally within us. For this reason Christians have long treasured the well-worn apostolic benediction in Hebrews 13:20–21.

> May the God of peace, who through the blood of the eternal covenant brought back from the dead our Lord Jesus, that great Shepherd of the sheep, equip you with everything good for doing his will, and may he work in us what is pleasing to him, through Jesus Christ, to whom be glory for ever and ever. Amen.

We need the God of peace to empower us to please him (see also Phil. 2:12–13; 3:10; 4:12–13).

Flowing from this, the Bible calls us to pray for this very divine power: "And we pray this in order that you may live a life worthy of the Lord and may please him in every way" (Col. 1:10). Praying for God's strength is the most practical demonstration of our felt need for it.

5. Jesus alone has fulfilled this pleasing-God goal perfectly. Jesus was the only perfect God pleaser who ever walked this earth—Jesus the beloved Son, the Son who perfectly pleased his Father, the Son in whom the Father was well pleased (John 4:34 with 17:4; see also Matt. 3:17; 17:5; Mark 1:11; Luke 3:22). While our failures to live up to the Lord's standards may discourage us, remember that ultimately it is not *our* God pleasing but Jesus's God pleasing that has satisfied God's perfect law and earned for us that saving righteousness that we could never secure. Only the doctrine of justification by grace through faith provides a sure foundation for our pursuit of God-pleasing obedience.

Implications of Pleasing God for Resolving Conflicts

What impact do these biblical principles about pleasing God have on our relationships? How do they shape the way we pursue peace? What will happen if we truly seek to please God? Consider nine far-reaching implications.

1. Failure to please God—our failure or the other person's, or both—is the ultimate cause of all relational conflict. Bank on it: whenever there is conflict, one or both parties are not pleasing God. In every marriage conflict, for example, you can assume that at least one spouse (likely both) is living to please himself or herself, and not the Lord. Marriage fights ultimately stem not from "incompatibility" or "personality differences," but from self-centeredness. Counselors commonly encounter married couples who blame various factors for their conflicts: family of origin, present circumstances, mental illness (proven or hypothesized), Satan, and so on. While factors like these can contribute to marital problems in varying degrees, they are not causative. They are influential but not determinative. The Bible resists dehumanizing people. We are God's image, not machines or robots. While computers might be susceptible to "garbage in, garbage out" problems, people have choices. Final causality for human behavior lies in each individual and his ongoing relationship with the living God. Marriage problems come because one or both parties disobey God's commands to please him by knowing, loving, serving, and forgiving his or her spouse.

2. This goal of pleasing God keeps our focus on God, not on the conflict issues or on the other person. In the midst of conflict, we tend to focus on the other person's sins ("I can't believe she said or did *that*"). We realign our goals and strategies in reference to that person. We attack, punish, or take revenge against him, or we defend ourselves, retreat, or avoid him. Our opponent consumes us. Our mind dwells on *his* actions. We rewind and replay mental videos of what he did. We reread mental transcripts of what he said. We review and rehearse in our minds the merits of our position and the weaknesses in the other person's argument.

However, when the goal of pleasing God captures us, it forces us to look upward, to pray, and to search God's Word. It forces us to look at God ("What does my Lord want me to do?") and at ourselves ("How have I contributed sinfully to the breakdown?"), and not at the other person. It drives us into God's Word to discern how he wants us to handle the situation.

3. In Christ, this goal is always doable, no matter how the other person behaves. In the midst of conflict, we often feel helpless. We can't control the circumstances, and we certainly can't control the other person. But with Christ's help there is something we can control: our responses. We are not helpless victims at the mercy of others. We have a goal that we can meet. It is always doable and achievable, no matter how the other person behaves. We can please God. The good news in conflict is that, even if the other person sins, we don't have to. There is not a person on the planet—including our most vicious enemy or the worst boss, roommate, or ex-spouse—who can stop us from pleasing our Lord! No news consoles us more than this when we are tempted to give up loving people who are hard to love.

4. This goal will help us pace our efforts (our energy, timing, risk, etc.). Most of us try to avoid conflict. We hate it. We fear it and run from it whenever possible. We delay talking to someone and find a dozen excuses for why the timing or setting is not right. For those who tend to withdraw, procrastinate, or avoid conflict, this goal of pleasing God will *push* us to do what we need to do without further delay. It will propel us forward to pursue peace. It will challenge us to see our avoidance as an unbiblical way to handle conflict and lead us to repent.

Some of us have the opposite problem. We are impatient, impetuous, and rash. We thrive on conflict. "Bring it on!" "Shoot first and ask questions later." The old maxim "Fools rush in where angels fear to tread" describes us too well. Reversing the counsel of James 1, we are slow to hear, quick to speak, and quick to become angry. We want to "sit down and talk it out, right now." What will this goal of pleasing God do for those who tend to act hastily or impulsively? It will *harness* us, forcing us to slow down, step back, and draw near to God first. It will challenge us to see our attacking as an unbiblical way to handle conflict, and it will lead us to repentance.

The lesson here is to know your own tendencies to either attack or run away. Joel and Karen are classic examples. They have their normal share of marital spats. But when they fail to deal with them gracefully, the drama begins. Joel pushes her to discuss an issue; Karen avoids the subject. Joel presses; Karen resists. Joel routinely says, "We need to sit down and talk"; Karen winces when she hears that line. Why? As she privately admitted to me, "I hate that expression. It always means that Joel wants to criticize me about something." On the other hand, Joel confided with me how frustrated he was that Karen never wanted to deal with important marital issues. And so their marriage limped along. What broke their logjam? Nothing less than this: a commitment by each of them, in response to a growing grasp of the gospel, to seek to please God. For Joel, it meant reviewing and repenting of his hasty and sometimes harsh ways of broaching important subjects. It meant letting go of minor offenses and learning to approach his wife in wiser ways on major matters. It meant talking to God before talking to Karen. For Karen, it meant reviewing and repenting of her fearful avoidance of Joel and learning to bring her fears to the Lord. It meant venturing forth, with conscious dependence on Jesus, to engage Joel on important matters and to consider the ways she has contributed to the relational rifts. It meant talking to God to ask him to help her talk to Joel.

5. God might bless our efforts by bringing reconciliation. The writer of Proverbs offers an encouraging perspective.

> When a man's ways are pleasing to the LORD,
> he makes even his enemies live at peace with him. (Prov. 16:7)

Your efforts to please God by loving the other person may open the door of reconciliation, either now or in the future. Of course, this is not guaranteed. The nature of a biblical proverb is that it is not an unconditional promise—Jesus, the perfect God pleaser, certainly did not experience peaceful responses from his enemies. Nevertheless, the Proverbs furnish us with Spirit-breathed observations about the way relationships often prosper when we do follow their wisdom.

Though not an absolute guarantee, this proverb envisions a possible outcome that can combat the hopelessness that too often controls our hearts during conflict: "He'll never change." "She will never respond to my efforts." To conclude this is to play the role of a modern prophet, making predictions that discount the power of God to change people. On what basis can we make such a *certain* (read *arrogant*) forecast? Has God given us some predictive insight unknown to everyone else? To mentally consign a now-hardened person to an entire lifetime of hard-heartedness betrays nothing less than unbelief in God's mighty, merciful hand. As long as our opponent has breath in this life, God's arm is not too short to reach him. His Spirit can melt icy hearts. While we have no guarantee that God will change the other person, we have no guarantee that he will not. While we must not seek to bargain with God ("I'll obey you, Lord, if you change him"), we can prayerfully ask God to use our God-pleasing efforts to soften and transform that person.

6. If both parties seek to please God, full reconciliation is guaranteed. If both parties please the Lord, relational restoration is not just possible; it is certain. Your marriage will grow. Your mother-daughter relationship will excel. Your separated husband and you will reunite. The sparring deacons will not precipitate a church split. Your son will repent of his rebellion. Your coworker and you will get along well. Despite your different backgrounds, incompatibilities, or personality differences, this dual commitment to Jesus will overcome all other obstacles.

Let me summarize what I often tell couples in my marriage counseling. Turning first to the husband (the order rarely matters), I will say: "Joel, I have some good news for you: If you seek to please God by following the biblical counsel I will give you, I can guarantee that *you* will become a more godly man, a more godly husband, and [if he has children] a more godly dad. But I can guarantee to you nothing about your *marriage*. Does that make sense?" I will then address the wife in the same way: "Karen, I have the same good news for you: If you seek to please God. . . ." Then I will address them both: "If, however, you *both* seek to please God by following the biblical counsel I will give you, then I can guarantee that not only will each of you become more godly as individuals, but your *marriage* will grow. That's God's assurance to you."

7. *Even if the other person does not please God, we can experience God's blessing and comfort.* Recall the realism we saw in chapter 1 from Romans 12:18: "If it is possible, as far as it depends on you, live at peace with everyone." While that verse calls us to pursue peace, it concurrently recognizes that it takes two to achieve reconciliation. God, of course, regularly reminds us that he blesses faithfulness, regardless of results. Consider, for example, Jesus's refrain in the parable of the ten talents: "His master replied, 'Well done, good and faithful servant! You have been faithful with a few things; I will put you in charge of many things. Come and share your master's happiness!'" (Matt. 25:21; cf. 1 Cor. 4:2–5; also John 8:29; 1 John 3:21–22). The consoling news for us is that even when others do not reciprocate our peacemaking efforts, we can hear God's voice, "Well done, good and faithful servant!"

8. *We must continue our commitments to please God even if the other person does not, and even if the relationship gets worse.* To be blunt, in the case of marriage, your relationship could get worse. The marital conflict can become a wakeup call for one spouse. He or she begins to pursue Christ with newfound love and energy, but the other spouse turns away from the Lord or gives up on the marriage. It is right at this point that we face the cost of discipleship. Nothing will test our commitment to follow the Lord more than this sad possibility. In the example of my words to Joel and Karen above, I might continue at some point with this question, "Are you each willing to commit yourselves to please God, whether or not your spouse does?"

This underscores another biblical truth: the only thing worse than being *in* a conflict is being *on the wrong side of* that conflict. That is why the apostle informs us, "No doubt there have to be differences among you to show which of you have God's approval" (1 Cor. 11:19).

While the presence of conflict may be unavoidable (recall our previous chapter), for the Christian, pleasing God in that conflict is not optional. Commitment to Jesus can divide marriages and families if our loved ones reject him and our pursuit of him (Matt. 10:32–39; Luke 14:25–27). A person's devotion to Jesus may not sit well with others. While such divisions are sad, God sometimes uses such to bring one true follower of Jesus out of two people who were merely drifting along in nominal Christianity. Our ultimate aim is to please God, not create peace apart from God. What matters supremely is not that you are in a conflict but that you are on God's side of the conflict.

9. *When the goal of pleasing God governs us, the other person's sins and failures become opportunities, not obstacles, to please God more and more, and to grow as a Christian.* Being in a relationship with a sinner, especially a repeat offender (as we all are), can be very difficult. And it is much easier to handle when we think that the tension will be temporary or that the person will change. Perhaps we and our friends begin to earnestly pray for the other person and we carry hope for his repentance. But what happens when we begin to conclude that this person may never change?

Essentially three options remain: (1) We can give up on pleasing God. (2) We can stoically and begrudgingly do the right thing, all the while cursing God under our breath for allowing this conflict to continue. Or (3) we can embrace the unpleasant situation as an opportunity given to us by our sovereign, wise, and good Father to make us more like Jesus, and we can pursue Jesus the Peacemaker and the greater joys he provides. We can remind ourselves that no one can stop us from pleasing God. And we can ask God to help us live for him.

Conclusion

Where do we start in pursuing peace? With a commitment to please God, in both our heart and our behavior. One tool that has helped me and others I have counseled is what I call "The Pleasing God Prayer":

> My goal in life, at all times, must be to *please God*, not myself or others. Father, in light of your grace, help me to please you in all my thoughts, words, actions, and desires.

Along with memorizing and meditating on 2 Corinthians 5:9 and 5:15, this focused prayer will help us fix our minds on the singular goal of pleasing God.

George Balanchine (1904–1983), one of the greatest twentieth-century choreographers, was the famed cofounder and longtime ballet master of the New York City Ballet Company. In *Between Walden and the Whirlwind*, Jean Fleming describes the relationship the dancers had with Balanchine, affectionately known to them as "Mr. B."

> To the dancers of the New York City Ballet Company, the late George Balanchine was both director and audience. They so loved, esteemed, and feared him, that no matter how large the crowds, they danced for only one audience: Mr. B. The enthusiastic applause from beyond the lights meant little if Mr. B. was not pleased.

Fleming then makes this insightful distinction: "To focus our life in Christ, we must allow Him to become our Director and Audience. The movements of our life must be choreographed by Him, performed for Him."[4] It is not enough for Jesus to be our director. He must also be our audience. We must not dance for the crowds or the *New York Times* theater critics but for Jesus, our "Mr. B."

What does this have to do with biblical peacemaking and our foundational first step of pleasing God? Everything. Most Christians understand that God must be their director, that they should seek to please God, and that Christian discipleship entails living under Jesus's lordship. We get that. The problem comes, however, when we fail to make him our audience. And so the frustrated, guilt-ridden man complains, "All my efforts to reason with my coworker haven't worked. I've failed." The depressed woman utters in despair, "I've tried hard to love my angry spouse, but it hasn't worked. He's still planning to file for divorce." Both of these people are living for Jesus as their director, but not as their audience. Their frustration, despair, and discontentment come because their audience—other people—are not pleased with their performance.

As our director, the Lord alone can dictate our behavior and call the shots. But that's not enough. He must also be our audience—the only one we seek to please, the one whose acceptance we most cherish, the

---

[4]Jean Fleming, *Between Walden and the Whirlwind* (Colorado Springs: NavPress, 1985), 24. I am grateful to Wayne Mack, a pastor, author, and biblical counselor, for this illustration.

one whose "well done, good and faithful servant" affirmation most satisfies, the one we play to supremely, and the only one whose smile or frown finally matters.

FOR PERSONAL REFLECTION OR GROUP DISCUSSION

1. What are some practical, specific ways you as an individual Christian can be sure that pleasing God and living for Christ are your single, all-consuming goal in life?

2. Which tendency do you tend to exhibit in conflict—avoiding or attacking? How can a commitment to please God alter that wrong tendency? How might it either push you or harness you to handle your conflicts differently?

3. Your friend is a Christian and confides in you concerning his (or her) side of a difficult conflict. You advise him to take certain wise steps. He begins to apply your suggestions but reports to you that things are not improving in the conflicted relationship, and he is ready to give up. What might you say to your friend to encourage him to please God and not give up his well-doing?

4. Study the following "pleasing God" passages and note insights and applications for each: John 5:30; 8:28–29; Romans 14:17–18; Ephesians 5:8–10; Colossians 1:10–12; 1 Thessalonians 4:1–2; 2 Timothy 2:3–4; and Hebrews 13:20–21. Then draft a three- or four-sentence summary of how these truths personally apply to you in any current conflict you face, and use that summary to guide you in asking God to help you.

5. Memorize and meditate daily on verses such as Psalm 19:14; 2 Corinthians 5:9, 15; and 2 Timothy 2:3–4, along with "The Pleasing God Prayer" noted above, and seek to apply them to any present conflict.

4

Getting to the Heart of Our Conflicts

What causes fights and quarrels among you?
Don't they come from your desires that battle within you?
James 4:1

You see, you spend a good piece of your life gripping a baseball,
and in the end it turns out that it was the other way around all the time.
Former major league pitcher Jim Bouton

Jessica became increasingly frustrated about her marriage, and understandably so. Her non-Christian husband, Nick, was an alcoholic, a womanizer, and a violent man. He spent his evenings shooting pool with his buddies at the bar, drinking, and fooling around with other women. All of Jessica's efforts to get him to stop never succeeded. Not even the arrival of their newborn daughter interrupted his lifestyle. He wanted no one—including God and especially his wife—to restrict his freedom. "I don't need another mother in my life," he frequently snapped. Jessica's efforts to change him regularly backfired and only provoked him to entrench himself more deeply into his patterns.

One evening, feeling especially frustrated and lonely, Jessica strapped her baby into her car seat and drove to the bar. She left the car idling, charged into the poolroom, and confronted Nick in front of his friends, accusing him of being an irresponsible husband and father. Nick exploded with anger, and with his pool cue in hand chased Jessica out of the bar to her car and smashed his stick on the windshield, cracking the glass and terrifying Jessica.

What drove Nick's rage? The same thing that drives anyone's sinful behavior: a sinful heart. All sinful behavior emerges from the remaining sin in our hearts. We will return to Nick and Jessica below, but first let's summarize the Bible's teaching about the heart.

A Biblical Look at Our Conflict-Causing Hearts

We begin with the timeless truth and the life-shaping priority found in Proverbs 4:23.

> Above all else, guard your heart,
> for it is the wellspring of life. (cf. 20:5)

The Path for Pursuing Peace

Step 1. Please God
Step 2. Repent
  A. Heart sins (beliefs, motives)
  B. Behavior sins (words, actions)
Step 3. Love the person

The timeless truth is that our heart is the center of our being; out of this wellspring everything else flows. The resultant life-shaping priority is to guard our heart, to diligently maintain its Godward posture. In Scripture, the heart is the intellectual, moral, spiritual, and emotional seat and control center of the entire inner person—what rules, drives, and controls us. It includes all our beliefs, motives, desires, emotions, affections, feelings, memories, will, intentions, and more, especially in relationship to God.[1] Hebrews 4:12, for example, speaks of "the thoughts and attitudes of the heart" (or "thoughts and intentions," ESV and NASB). That is why the appeal in Proverbs 23:26, "My son, give me your heart," carries such force. If God has my heart, he has me!

Deuteronomy 8:2 tells us that exposing the Israelites' hearts was part of God's agenda for their desert wandering: "Remember how the LORD your God led you all the way in the desert these forty years, to

---

[1] *Heart* is "the richest biblical term for the totality of man's inner or immaterial nature. In biblical literature it is the most frequently used term for man's immaterial personality functions as well as the most inclusive term for them since, in the Bible, virtually every immaterial function of man is attributed to the 'heart.'" Andrew Bowling, "1071 לֵבָב," in *Theological Wordbook of the Old Testament*, ed. R. Laird Harris, Gleason L. Archer Jr., and Bruce K. Waltke (Chicago: Moody Press, 1999), 466. See also entries for "Heart" in standard Bible references works, e.g., Walter A. Elwell, *Evangelical Dictionary of Biblical Theology* (Grand Rapids: Baker, 1997), and Leland Ryken, Jim C. Wilhoit, Tremper Longman III, eds., *Dictionary of Biblical Imagery* (Downers Grove, IL: InterVarsity, 2000).

humble you and to test you in order to know what was in your heart, whether or not you would keep his commands."

The prophet Ezekiel likewise understood Israel's heart problem. In Ezekiel 11:19–20 God promised new hearts to his true people: "I will give them an undivided heart and put a new spirit in them; I will remove from them their heart of stone and give them a heart of flesh. Then they will follow my decrees and be careful to keep my laws." The alternative in verse 21 is a tragic warning: "But as for those whose hearts are devoted to their vile images and detestable idols, I will bring down on their own heads what they have done."

In Ezekiel 14:3 God reveals to his prophet the current heart condition of Israel's exiled elders: "Son of man, these men have set up idols in their hearts and put wicked stumbling blocks before their faces." But God will not tolerate their renewed idolatry. He promises to confront his people. Why? God answers in verse 5, "I will do this to recapture the hearts of the people of Israel, who have all deserted me for their idols." He then issues his call to thorough repentance in verse 6, "Repent! Turn from your idols. . . ."

God yearns to recapture people's hearts. In coaching those in conflict, I have often wished that I could somehow take their hearts in my hand and gently turn them in a Godward direction. Or to switch the metaphor, I have wished that I could adjust their hearts to receive God's life-changing transmission, the way I used to adjust the rabbit-ear antennae on my first television set.

The theme continues in Ezekiel 18:31, where the prophet calls out to his hearers, "Rid yourselves of all the offenses you have committed, and get a new heart and a new spirit." The matter then resolves in Ezekiel's new covenant promise in 36:25–27 with God's ultimate answer.

> I will sprinkle clean water on you, and you will be clean; I will cleanse you from all your impurities and from all your idols. I will give you a new heart and put a new spirit in you; I will remove from you your heart of stone and give you a heart of flesh. And I will put my Spirit in you and move you to follow my decrees and be careful to keep my laws.

What we cannot do—change or cleanse our own hearts—God has done for us through Jesus Christ and his Holy Spirit.

Jesus continues and intensifies the prophets' concerns. In Matthew 12:34, he confronts the Jewish leaders and shows that their sinful speech arises from their evil hearts: "You brood of vipers, how can you who are evil say anything good? For out of the overflow of the heart the mouth speaks." In Matthew 15:18–19, Jesus explains to his disciples that "the things that come out of the mouth come from the heart, and these make a man 'unclean.' For out of the heart come evil thoughts, murder, adultery, sexual immorality, theft, false testimony, slander." Sinful behavior flows from a sinful heart.

James (and You and Me)

With this general biblical background of the heart's role in generating behavior, we turn to the epistle of James to help us understand the cause of conflicts between Nick and Jessica. In James 4, the writer explicitly addresses relational conflicts.[2] And he does so in a piercing way by examining their source: "What causes fights and quarrels among you?" (v. 1). I have often wondered how I might have written verse 1. I'm afraid it would have looked more like this: "Brothers, I hear there are fights and quarrels among you. . . . STOP IT! And go to your room, right now!" But moralism doesn't work. It disheartens, discourages, and drains us. Commands to "stop fighting!" don't stop people from fighting. Telling two people to "just kiss and make up" or "hug it out" reconciles no one. Reconciliation is not merely about anger management, changing bad habits, or five tips for fair fighting.

That's why I like the Bible. And that's why I like James. James is not short on commands; his letter is loaded with short, sharp, proverb-like admonitions. And he certainly wants us to stop fighting and start reconciling. But James is equally concerned about bringing thorough and lasting change. He knows that mere moralism, behaviorism, or externalism is not God's way.

Therefore, James addresses conflict in a more profound way. Like Proverbs, Moses, the Prophets, and Jesus above, he addresses our hearts. His answer to his own rhetorical question brings penetrating insight. "What causes fights and quarrels among you?" He pinpoints their cause:

---

[2]I addressed this passage and similar themes in chaps. 3–4 in my book, *Uprooting Anger: Biblical Help for a Common Problem* (Phillipsburg, NJ: P&R, 2005).

"Don't they come from your desires that battle within you? You want something but don't get it. You kill and covet, but you cannot have what you want. You quarrel and fight" (4:1b–2a). The apostle understands that sinful behavior comes from the heart. Sinful desires breed sinful conflicts, quarrels, and fights.

But in what way are desires sinful? What kind of desires produce fights and quarrels? One way to answer that would be to list all sorts of sinful items—evil things, forbidden objects—that someone might desire. Yet I have found in my many years of pastoral counseling that these rarely drive personal conflicts.

There's another way to understand how desires can be evil and can cause conflicts. While James does not tell us what his readers desired— some commentators suggest money—he does not say the object itself was evil or forbidden. In fact, James holds out the possibility that God our Father—our good Father—might even give it to his readers. Verse 2 ends with the observation, "You do not have, because you do not ask God." I infer from this that the desired object is not inherently sinful but that if you ask God (v. 2) and if you ask for it unselfishly (v. 3), then God might give it to you if it is his will (v. 16; cf. 1 John 5:14 and similar prayer texts). God would never give us something that is evil. Our holy and good God (James 1:13, 17; cf. Matt 7:9–11) will not answer prayer for a successful bank robbery.

So if the problem is not with the object, what is it? In verse 1 James says that conflicts come from our desires that "battle" within us. James uses military imagery to picture desires at war, desires that are encamped, entrenched, and established in our hearts. Historically, pastoral theologians have called these desires "inordinate desires"— desires that rule me, that are too important, that are out of order, and that dominate our hearts. We don't just want something, *we've got to have it!* We want it too much, too desperately. And when we don't get what we want, we fight and quarrel.

This one insight opens a world of understanding about the cause of conflict. It is not just evil things like illegal drugs or stolen money but good things that become mini-gods to me. What are the kinds of things—perhaps good things in and of themselves—that can rule our hearts? I "need/must have"

- a husband who loves me, as I am, unconditionally,
- a boss who notices me, appreciates me, and commends my work,
- a child who loves me and respects me,
- a dad who will spend time with me,
- a wife who fulfills me sexually (or who doesn't want sex),
- a pastor who will visit me or teach on topics I think we need to hear,
- a neighbor who will muzzle his barking dog,
- a son who achieves good grades, takes out the trash, and so forth,
- a coach who plays me enough,
- a teacher who grades me fairly,
- a roommate who picks up his clothes and cleans our kitchen sink,
- a department of highways who will complete that road project.

What do you notice about each desired item above? None of them is inherently evil. In fact, most, if not all, are things that God would want the other person to give. The problem is that these desires have become heart-controlling desires. And the list of candidates is endless. We can demand from others affection, attention, approval, admiration, acceptance, and appreciation (and that's just a list that starts with *A*!). When we demand these things, conflict will surely arise.

James, Nick, and Jessica (and You and Me)

Let's return to Nick and Jessica. What inordinate, "James 4" desires created Nick's rage? At first Nick enjoyed the freedoms and benefits—the good things—that a wife provided. But in time the challenges, burdens, and duties of marriage and parenting began to overwhelm him. His desires for convenience, pleasure, and independence started to rule him. He treasured the good feelings—albeit temporary and often diminishing—that came from his buddies, his affairs, and his alcohol. Nick did not want anyone to rule him, especially a woman (yes, add chauvinism to the above mix). His cravings for freedom and convenience—mixtures of good and bad things initially in Nick's confused soul—eventually gave way to the explicitly evil acts of adultery, drunkenness, and violence.

Divorce seemed inevitable. Yet Nick didn't want a divorce—not because he wanted to work on his marriage, but because he didn't want to disappoint his grandmother by adding another divorce to her grandchildren's records. Besides, there were benefits to having a Christian wife who cared for him, cooked for him, cleaned his clothes, and often gave him sex when he wanted it. But his heart echoed the language of the unruly subjects in Jesus's parable of the king: "But his subjects hated him and sent a delegation after him to say, 'We don't want this man to be our king'" (Luke 19:14). Apart from a new heart and radical repentance, Nick would not be able to control his rage and lusts, and love his wife in God-pleasing ways.

But what about Jessica? Was Nick the only player in their conflict? Did she contribute to the incident above and to the similar patterns they experienced? What led her to leave her apartment that night to travel to a bar to "rescue" her husband, embarrass him in front of all his friends, and provoke his chronic anger to become violent? To even ask the question might offend some,[3] so I will let Jessica share her answer to the question: "As I have looked back at these and similar episodes through a biblical lens, I now see that my own desires were also sinful. Less obvious, less dramatic, and less destructive of people or property, but no less sinful." On the surface her desires all seemed innocent, understandable, and commendable. "I just wanted a closer relationship with Nick. I still loved him. And I wanted him home with me each night, the way it was when we first married. I wanted him to enjoy our daughter with me as she grows up. I wanted him to just spend time with us. And maybe even have another baby or two. That's why I pressured and nagged and called him out in front of his friends."

Can anyone fault Jessica for these desires? She wanted a husband who would love her, care for her, be a good dad, not get drunk, and keep his marriage vows to forsake other women and be faithful to her. Are these not the desires that God wants her as a Christian wife to have for her husband? Yes. And are these not the desires that God himself has for Nick? Yes. These are outcomes she should hope for, pray for, and affirm if or when she sees evidence of them.

But for Jessica they were more than desires for good things. They became demands. How do we know? Three tests can help us detect

---

[3] I do not mean to lessen the severity of spousal abuse or to imply that Jessica was in any way responsible for Nick's violence or other related sins. But I do mean to state that Jessica is fully responsible for her own heart and behavior before God, and that God had a growth agenda for Jessica during this difficult period in her life.

when a desire for a good thing has become an inordinate, ruling desire—a James 4:1–3 type of demand:

- *Does it consume my thoughts?* Do I obsess about it? Does my mind drift to it when I don't have to think about other things (like when I am showering)?
- *Do I sin to get it?* Do I manipulate people or situations to get what I want? Do I bargain or nag or try a guilt trip?
- *Do I sin when I don't get it?* Do I pout or explode or pull away or gossip about someone when he or she doesn't give me my desired thing?

Measured by these marks, Jessica's desires were indeed inordinate. Not always, of course. There were many days when she learned to entrust herself, Nick, and her daughter into God's hands, and she handled her hardships in God-delighting ways. (And in the process she greatly encouraged my faith and the faith of those who knew and loved her!)

On the occasion noted above, however, Jessica crossed the line. "I was very down spiritually that day," she recalls. "I felt lonely and was not resting in God's love for me. I was filled with self-pity. And as I thought about Nick being there with his friends, I decided to give him a piece of my mind. I knew it was wrong but I didn't care. I was tired of the life Nick was leaving me with. And I wanted his friends to know what he was doing to me."

The formula for a perfect marital storm was in place: an insensitive, demanding husband prone to violence + a lonely, demanding wife desperate enough to provoke her husband on his turf = violence and disaster. In marriage, when legitimate (or illegitimate) desires become entrenched, ruling demands, and when they remain unmet, fights will ensue. If these patterns continue, they will lead ultimately to further violence or separation and divorce.

Ken Sande supplies a simple summary of how these heart dynamics give birth to actual conflict. Sande calls it "The Progression of an Idol" and teaches a four-step model.[4]

---

[4]Ken Sande, *The Peacemaker: A Biblical Guide to Resolving Personal Conflict*, 3rd ed. (Grand Rapids: Baker, 2004), chap. 5. I have inserted arrows to mark the progression that Sande's model presents. Sande acknowledges his appreciation for the Christian Counseling and Educational Foundation and its past and present faculty (e.g., David Powlison, Ed Welch, Paul David Tripp, and John Bettler) for these heart-related insights.

I desire Õ I demand Õ I judge Õ I punish

While my initial desire might be legitimate, it becomes sinful when it becomes a demand. And when it becomes a demand and you don't meet it—and of course you can never meet every demand of my selfish heart—I then judge you in my heart and condemn you. Then in the final step my internal judgment produces some outward expression of punishment toward you on the behavioral level. I might yell at you, speak sarcastically about you, gossip about you, or avoid you.

The Throne-Staircase Diagram

One tool I frequently use in conflict coaching is the throne-staircase diagram (fig. 2). The throne itself represents your heart. The cross represents Jesus Christ, who rules on the heart throne of the Christian. The letters under the throne signify specific desires. The placement of the desires *under* the throne is significant. In a well-ordered life that follows Jesus, our desires—whether met or unmet—are submitted and subordinated to Jesus. In fact, a large part of the art of living for Jesus is learning to live contentedly with ongoing unmet desires. When my desires remain submitted to Christ, my soul finds rest. Inner peace reigns.

Figure 2. The throne-staircase diagram: desires submitted

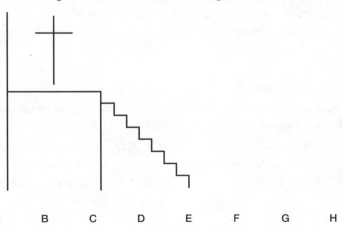

A   B   C   D   E   F   G   H

What happens when a desire begins to grow and become inordinate? As we see in figure 3, the desire sprouts a pair of legs and begins to ascend the staircase, rising to the top of the throne to compete with Jesus for lordship of my heart.

Figure 3. The throne-staircase diagram: desires becoming demands

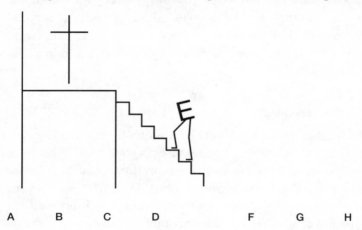

A   B   C   D   F   G   H

Left unchecked, any desire has the potential to climb the stairs in an effort to overthrow and remove Jesus. The flesh in my Spirit-versus-flesh civil war (Gal. 5:16–26; 1 Pet. 2:11–12) continually plots a *coup d'état* against King Jesus as my rightful Lord. Apart from grace the remnant sin in my heart would overthrow my enthroned King.

How does God want us to handle our desires that grow into demands? A simple alliterated outline provides a plan: Recognize, Repent, Refocus, and Replace.

1. Recognize the Ascending Desire

The first step is to recognize which specific desire tends to ascend to your throne, become a demand, and control you—and to catch it when it starts this ascent. Our goal is to become increasingly "heart smart"—to seize the first occasion of a rising desire and to call it what it is. The three tests mentioned above may help you: (1) Does it consume my thoughts? (2) Do I sin to get it? (3) Do I sin when I don't get it?

You may also find it helpful to complete the following sample statements. Any of these can help you unearth your conflict-causing demands; together they can capture various nuances:

- *"You must give me ___ or I'll be angry at you or cold toward you or . . ."*
- *"If only ___ would change, I would be satisfied or content."* (See below for ways Jessica applied Phil. 4:11–13 regarding contentment.)
- *"If I don't get ___, then I become depressed, angry, or anxious."*
- *"What I think I need or I desperately want is ___."* (For a biblical view of our ultimate needs, see Pss. 27:4, 10; 73:23–28; Matt. 4:4; Luke 10:38–42; 2 Pet. 1:3.)

John Bettler, the former executive director of the Christian Counseling and Educational Foundation and professor of practical theology at Westminster Theological Seminary, stated the last one this way: "A person has power over you to the extent that he has something you think you need or something that you desperately want."

This insight exposed Jessica's heart. To the degree that she wrongly believed that she *needed* a changed Nick to experience true joy, peace, and contentment, Jessica was enslaved. "Jessica," I explained, "in many ways you are like the wooden spool at the end of a yo-yo string, hanging on Nick's finger. When he treats you nicely, you're up—you come to our counseling sessions happy and hopeful. When he treats you rudely, you're down—you come to our sessions bummed, depressed, or angry. Your yo-yo like emotions come because you have placed your life on Nick's finger, allowing him to control your heart by the way he treats you. You have given him the power to raise you up or hurl you down, all because you wrongly believe that you need him to change. Jesus wants to free you from that slavery. His Word and his Spirit can liberate you, and I can help you find that freedom in Christ. As you find the inner stability Jesus has for you, Jessica, you will still experience degrees of sadness if Nick does not follow the Lord. But all that will be tempered by a deepening sense within you of joy, peace, and confidence that Jesus provides."

2. Repent of Letting the Desire Rule

As we have seen in various passages above, repentance is the frequent call from the Lord to those who struggle with sins in the heart. Here we must be keenly specific: For what do we repent? For our desires? No, the desires are not the problem. In fact, having desires is good—they remind us to pray, to submit ourselves to God, to seek godly directions, and so forth. We must not try to deaden, neuter, or deny our legitimate desires. Instead, we must repent not of the desire but of the "ruling-ness" of the desire, that is, the way it has begun to ascend the throne and become a demand. The desire itself is not the evil in view; it is the propensity for it to climb and take over that we must resist.

Whenever we consider repentance, we must keep one vital truth uppermost in our thinking. God always calls for repentance in response to grace already given. Joel 2 powerfully illustrates this truth.

> "Even now," declares the LORD,
>> "return to me with all your heart,
>> with fasting and weeping and mourning."
> Rend your heart
>> and not your garments.
> Return to the LORD your God,
>> for he is gracious and compassionate,
> slow to anger and abounding in love,
>> and he relents from sending calamity. (vv. 12–13)

Here, in a context preceding God's judgment, the prophet offers hope. While he calls for deep repentance—a thoroughly ripped heart that returns to God—verse 13 includes a key word we must not miss: "for." To clarify this truth, I like to ask counselees which came first: the call to repentance (with God then becoming gracious to those who repent) or God being gracious (with repentance to be done in light of that)? Based on the word "for," the answer is the latter. God does not become gracious only after we repent. He already "*is* gracious and compassionate," and this becomes the ground that encourages us to come to him—whether in initial conversion or repeatedly in ongoing fellowship with Christ.

In other words, whether it is the initial gospel call of John 3:16 or the ongoing dynamic of Christian living, in God's economy his provision and promise of grace always precede his call to faith and repentance. The Westminster Shorter Catechism's answer to question 87, "What is repentance unto life?," is especially instructive: "Repentance unto life is a saving grace, whereby a sinner, out of a true sense of his sin, and *apprehension of the mercy of God in Christ*, doth, with grief and hatred of his sin, turn from it unto God, with full purpose of, and endeavor after, new obedience" (emphasis added). In all gospel-driven repentance, the apprehension of God's mercy in Christ motivates us to turn back to God. We will never truly turn back to a God we doubt will receive us; we will go to a God who loves us and will accept us because of Jesus.

The same dynamic appears in Hebrews 4:14–16, where the provision of Jesus as our High Priest furnishes motivation for us to hold firmly to him and the new covenant he has brought, and to come to God's throne of grace.

> Therefore, since we have a great high priest who has gone through the heavens, Jesus the Son of God, let us hold firmly to the faith we profess. For we do not have a high priest who is unable to sympathize with our weaknesses, but we have one who has been tempted in every way, just as we are—yet was without sin. Let us then approach the throne of grace with confidence, so that we may receive mercy and find grace to help us in our time of need.

The provisions here are rich: We have a great high priest who has gone not through an earthly curtain (alluding to Leviticus 16) but through the heavenly places into the very presence of God, into the eternal Holy of Holies, not to offer animals but to offer himself as God's final atoning sacrifice for us. He is a mighty Savior—"the Son of God." Moreover, he feels our weaknesses and temptations, yet because he has not succumbed to them (he is "without sin") he can both sympathize with us and concurrently enable us to resist sin and not revert back to our old ways. And when we come to God's throne of grace, we will find forgiving grace ("mercy") and enabling, empowering grace ("grace to help us in our time of need").

This means that there is always a way back to God for anyone—be it Nick or Jessica, or you or me. Liberation for Jessica began when she saw how her demanding heart was ruining her relationship with Nick. I offered her an analogy: "Jessica, if I would *like* my wife to admire me, but she doesn't, I will be disappointed. But if I *need* her to do so, but she doesn't, I will be crushed. The difference in whether I will be merely disappointed (or bummed or sad) or crushed (or paralyzed or enraged)

69

has nothing to do with my wife's behavior. It has everything to do with me. It entirely depends on what I bring to the relationship: if I would *like* her admiration or if I wrongly think I *need* her admiration." Jessica readily saw the distinction; her felt needs had hijacked her heart and had driven her toward alternating rage and despair.

3. Refocus on God and His Grace, Provisions, and Promises

Third, we should refocus our hearts by resubmitting our desires under the throne of Jesus's lordship and fastening our eyes on God's presence and promises in our life. This includes a recommitment to please, adore, trust, and obey him. In a short, condensed insertion, James 4:6 puts it this way:

> But he gives us more grace. That is why Scripture says:
>
> > "God opposes the proud
> > but gives grace to the humble."

For Nick, this would mean a radical conversion to Christ, turning from idols to the living God (1 Thess. 1:9–10), something that never happened to my knowledge during the time I worked with them. Nick needed a Redeemer, and he refused the one that Jessica and I offered.

For Jessica, this involved resetting her heart on God himself as her sole sufficiency. "Through all this I came to realize that I was wrongly building my life on Nick and on the identity of being married, and not being a daughter of God." Several passages especially helped Jessica and formed the foundation for her refocused view of God and his provisions for her:

> His divine power has given us everything we need for life and godliness through our knowledge of him who called us by his own glory and goodness. Through these he has given us his very great and precious promises, so that through them you may participate in the divine nature and escape the corruption in the world caused by evil desires. (2 Pet. 1:3–4)

Jessica was especially strengthened by the promise that in Christ she truly had all she needed, however Nick treated her.

> "Martha, Martha," the Lord answered, "you are worried and upset about many things, but only one thing is needed. Mary has chosen what is better, and it will not be taken away from her." (Luke 10:41–42)

Jessica's one word response: "Guilty! But thankful for a patient Savior who is the one stable thing in my life that cannot be removed."

> One thing I ask of the LORD,
>   this is what I seek:
> that I may dwell in the house of the LORD
>   all the days of my life,
> to gaze upon the beauty of the LORD
>   and to seek him in his temple. (Ps. 27:4)

The simplicity of the "one thing" vision captured Jessica, especially as she reflected on Jesus as her new temple, the meeting place for her and God through his cross.

> Though my father and mother forsake me,
>   the LORD will receive me. (Ps. 27:10)

Jessica substituted the phrase "my husband" in her prayers and meditations on this text, and she saw how she had too often focused on the seen reality of a husband who forsook her and not the unseen greater reality of a Redeemer who received her.

> Yet I am always with you;
>   you hold me by my right hand.
> You guide me with your counsel,
>   and afterward you will take me into glory.
> Whom have I in heaven but you?
>   And earth has nothing I desire besides you.
> My flesh and my heart may fail,
>   but God is the strength of my heart
>   and my portion forever. (Ps. 73:23–26)

Jessica mourned over the fact that her desires were far too Nick-centered. She also drew comfort from the last verse that even in her failings her God was gracious, powerful, and sufficient on her behalf.

> I am not saying this because I am in need, for I have learned to be content whatever the circumstances. I know what it is to be in need, and I know what it is to have plenty. I have learned the secret of being content in any and every situation, whether well fed or hungry, whether living in plenty or in want. I can do everything through him who gives me strength. (Phil. 4:11–13)

Applying Paul's model to her relational poverty, Jessica embarked on the progressive path of learning contentment, even in her adverse marital circumstances, "through him who gives me strength."

4. Replace Sinful Responses with Christlike Graces

The final step is continual and ongoing. God calls us in progressive ways to replace the previously ascending but now resubmitted desires with fresh, ongoing replacements: relational graces (we'll consider Eph. 4:1–3 and Col. 3:12–14 in chap. 7), good works (Eph. 2:10; Titus 3:14), and Spirit-generated fruit (Gal. 5:22–23; Col. 1:9–12). While the specifics must be tailored to each individual, they often include learning contentment, self-control, prayer, biblical peacemaking, forgiveness, godly listening, godly speaking, and the ninefold fruit of the Holy Spirit.

For Jessica, this meant change and growth in several specific areas: (1) learning contentment (finding her identity as God's daughter more than as Nick's wife), (2) self-control (no more sudden trips to the bar to frantically find her carousing husband and holding her tongue when tempted to blast Nick for his sin), (3) godly speaking (knowing when to gently share, opine, or inquire without nagging, condemning, or provoking), and (4) controlling her own daydreaming about what it would be like to be married to a godly man. As she continued in counseling and in a small-group setting with a Christ-centered mutual-ministry agenda, we saw great progress.

May God grant us all by his Spirit the kind of heart repentance that his Word commands, that Nick needs, and that Jessica joyfully tastes.

FOR PERSONAL REFLECTION OR GROUP DISCUSSION

1. Mention some natural or legitimate desires that you have that can easily climb your heart throne to become ruling desires or demands.

2. When one of those desires becomes enthroned, how might it lead you to some form of conflict with others? What does that look like? And what do you think God would want you to do about it?

3. In what ways does our culture encourage the desires-that-become-demands problem? This may include the use of contemporary cultural synonyms like *wants*, *needs*, *rights*, *demands*, as well as *deserve*, and related language. For example, consider advertising and TV commercials as powerful avenues through which our culture screams the desires and demands of the human heart.

5

Owning Our Sins before God Our Savior

The line dividing good and evil cuts through the heart of every human being.

Aleksandr Solzhenitsyn

You have not yet considered how great your sin is.

St. Anselm

For I know my transgressions,
and my sin is always before me.
Against you, you only, have I sinned
and done what is evil in your sight.

Psalm 51:3–4

He didn't mean to do it. He had never done it before. And thankfully he hasn't done it since. But he did do it. And it was bad. It all happened swiftly—almost spontaneously—amid a heated argument. His frustration mounted, she shot a stinging remark, and he slapped her across the face. Roy knew immediately that he was wrong, and he felt horrible. He quickly told Sonya that he was sorry, that he felt really bad, and that he would never do it again.

They made up that night and the incident passed undiscussed. Sonya's physical pain was minimal; it passed quickly with no injury. But the relational slap went deeper. Like most couples married for many years, Roy and Sonya had experienced their normal share of conflicts. But this was the low point in their marital journey. Both would attest that after that point their marriage had never been quite the same. It limped for years.

Eventually they came to their pastor for marriage counseling over what they called "communication problems." As the pastor gathered their marital history, Roy mentioned the incident. His guilt seemed to

74

linger, but he added a note of frustration. "Pastor," Roy said, "I didn't mean to do it. And I apologized to her. I told her I was sorry. But she still seems mad about this. Sonya has never forgiven me."

Such a scenario frequently recurs in all sorts of relationships. A coworker speaks rudely to others, and then feels bad and apologizes, but it doesn't seem to "take," and the office tension continues. A church leader fails in some specific way to care for a needy member. He tells the member that he is sorry, and the member tells him that it's okay. But the member remains distant, and the pastor stays in that member's doghouse until one of them leaves the church. A mother scolds her teenage daughter harshly. She apologizes and makes successful strides in controlling her tongue, but the daughter seems cool toward her for many months. Their relationship never improves.

What is happening in these cases? When we hear about broken relationships, we typically assume that the fault lies chiefly with the party who fails to forgive. In other words, we take reported apologies at face value, as acceptable givens. We then assume that if a breach remains, then it must be due to unforgiveness by the offended party. The offender himself frequently thinks this: "I said I was sorry, but he never forgave me." "I sought her forgiveness, but she still hasn't let it go."

Why is this a mistake? It is certainly not because forgiveness is unimportant. Far from it; as we will see in chapters 8–9, forgiveness is crucial for many reasons. A failure to forgive will keep the conflict alive. No, the mistake lies in assuming that all apologies are of equal value. We forget that a solid confession is needed to initiate a solid confession-forgiveness dynamic. In other words, confession carries a logical priority over forgiveness. No relationship—marital, parental, or otherwise—will flourish if an offended partner doubts the offender's sorrow or his willingness to take responsibility for his actions. To reconcile an injured relationship we need *both* a solid confession of sin and a solid declaration of forgiveness.

Why is confession so important? And what makes a confession

The Path for Pursuing Peace

Step 1. Please God
Step 2. Repent
   A. Heart sins (beliefs, motives)
   B. Behavior sins (words, actions)
Step 3. Love the person

---

solid—one that pleases God and makes it easier for the offended party to forgive the offender and reconcile the relationship?

Consider Jesus's words in the Sermon on the Mount in Matthew 7:3–5. To set the context, Jesus appears in Matthew 1–2 as the Son of Abraham, the Son of David, and the Son of God, fulfilling the messianic promises of the Hebrew Scriptures. He will save us from our sins (the meaning of the name "Jesus," 1:21) and be with us (the meaning of "Immanuel," 1:23). In Matthew 3–4 he is the divine Son of God who has withstood in a concentrated way the temptations that God's son Israel did not withstand. He has overcome Satan on our behalf, he has brought God's kingdom to earth, and he now calls everyone to repent and follow him. Then, in Matthew 5–7, in light of this kingdom victory and saving promises, he rises as our new Lawgiver and Prophet to outline the radically new lifestyle he commands for us as his followers.

Key Truths from Matthew 7:3–5

In the opening verses of Matthew 7 Jesus warns against judging others in ungodly ways.[1] Then he asks some probing questions in verses 3–5.

> Why do you look at the speck of sawdust in your brother's eye and pay no attention to the plank in your own eye? How can you say to your brother, "Let me take the speck out of your eye," when all the time there is a plank in your own eye? You hypocrite, first take the plank out of your own eye, and then you will see clearly to remove the speck from your brother's eye.

Let me draw four observations about this passage.

1. By a "plank" Jesus refers to our sinful behavior. Jesus evidently refers to wrong actions that are visible to others, actions that render us hypocrites if we criticize the sins of others. Our planks refer to our

---

[1]People sometimes cite Matt. 7:1 as an absolute prohibition against all forms of judgment. But this misses Jesus's point and contradicts other New Testament teaching. There are proper times for judging and discerning. In the very same context, vv. 5–6, 15–20 require us to assess someone's sins and respond appropriately. In John 7:24, Jesus exhorts his listeners to "stop judging by mere appearances, and make a right judgment" (see also Matt. 18:15–17; 1 Cor. 5:11–13). In Matt. 7:1 Jesus condemns the hypocritical judging pictured in vv. 2–5. See also chap. 10 below.

behavioral sins—observable by others—both our sinful words (including our facial expressions and grunts) and our sinful actions. Some writers wisely distinguish heart sins and social sins.[2] God calls us to confess to him all sins but to confess to others only our social sins, our sins that people might witness. In other words, God does not call me to confess to someone, "I am jealous of you," or "I lust sexually for you" (heart sins), but only my words or actions (social sins) that might arise from them.

How should we determine our "plank" sins? The standard to measure this, of course, is Scripture. The Bible alone—nothing more or less—defines what sin is. God does not permit us to raise (by legalism) or lower (by license) the Bible's bar. Nor is ignorance an excuse: "I didn't know it was sinful" does not mean it was not sinful. Nor can we passively sit back and wait for God to convict us of our sin if the Bible plainly calls it sinful. God's Word, not our conscience or subjective feelings, remains our final standard.

Furthermore, we need to expand our definition of planks to include sins of both commission and omission. Commission sins involve words or actions that I say or do but I *should not* say or do. Omission sins involve words or actions that I do not say or do but *should*. First John 3:4 describes the first: "Everyone who sins breaks the law; in fact, sin is lawlessness"; James 4:17 warns against the second: "Anyone, then, who knows the good he ought to do and doesn't do it, sins." The Westminster Shorter Catechism summarizes this dual perspective in a simple sentence: "Sin is any want of conformity unto, or transgression of, the law of God."[3] When I fail to conform to God's law (omission), or when I transgress God's law (commission), I sin. We find the same commission-omission dynamic in various prayer liturgies, like this line from the Episcopal *Book of Common Prayer*: "Most merciful God, we confess that we have sinned against you in thought, word, and deed, by what we have done, and by what we have left undone." Using examples of marital conflict, figure 4 pictures these possibilities in four quadrants, including both the words and actions that I sinfully commit or omit.

---

[2] Jay E. Adams, *A Theology of Christian Counseling: More Than Redemption* (1979; Grand Rapids: Zondervan, 1986), 218ff.
[3] Answer to question 14, "What is sin?"

Figure 4. The "Plank" Commission-Omission Assessment

	Commission	Omission	
Words	A husband yells at his wife.	A husband fails to ask his wife how she is doing after a pressure-filled day.	Words
Actions	A husband hits his wife.	A husband forgets to give his wife a birthday gift.	Actions
	Commission	Omission	

Roy's hitting his wife is an obvious bottom-left sin, while his and Sonya's heated words belong in the upper-left quadrant. Yet their failure to speak positively—their neglecting grace and kindness—are upper-right sins that have likewise injured their marriage. In fact, most marital sins among Christians fall into the omission column, and these can hurt even more deeply than commission sins. Even if we don't yell at each other, we may simply fail to speak and act in loving, Christlike ways toward each other. While I have never hit my wife, on too many occasions I have failed to enter her world with caring concern. While I have never attacked a fellow church member, I have failed to reach out to some members or shepherd them as well as I could have.

Finally, to assess what our planks are, it is wise to examine our sinful behavior at various points in the conflict—before, during, and after:

- What sinful words or actions did I say or do *before* our conflict that helped provoke or set the stage for it?
- What were my sins of commission and omission *during* the heat of our conflict?
- What "plank" sins did I evidence *after* the conflict that have helped keep it alive and unresolved?

I might not have started the clash, but my sinful responses might have prolonged or escalated it.

2. Jesus presents the proper order: You must start with you. With two piercing questions, Jesus masterfully uncovers the way we ignore our own sins and dwell on how others have wronged us: "Why do you look at the speck of sawdust in your brother's eye and pay no attention to the plank in your own eye? How can you say to your brother, 'Let me take the speck out of your eye,' when all the time there is a plank in your own eye?" (Matt. 7:3–4). He then hammers home the point in verse 5: "You hypocrite, *first* take the plank out of your own eye, and then you will see clearly to remove the speck from your brother's eye." Focus on your sins first.

Jesus uses an exaggeration to make his point. Imagine going to an optometrist's office for an eye exam. You arrive at the doctor's office and his assistant does the usual vision check. You then wait to see the doctor. Can you imagine what you would do if your optometrist entered the examination room with a huge hunk of cherry wood protruding from his right eye? "Physician, heal yourself!" would be my first thought as I scrambled to get out of there! He can't work on my eyes if he has not dealt with his own.

The question, therefore, that flows from this passage is piercing: *Whose sins bother you more—your sins or the other person's*? It's amazing to me how often I can walk away from a fight with my wife and mutter more about what she said or did than my own contribution. "I can't believe she said that" more frequently flows through my mind than "I can't believe I said that." I have little doubt that a video recording of my last conflict with Lauren would provide plenty of footage of my own sinful behavioral planks.

Of course, all this assumes that we are willing to look at our sins and to own our guilt before God and others. That's what Jesus calls each one of us to do, since "God opposes the proud but gives grace to the humble" (James 4:6). The most riveting illustration of this truth comes in Jesus's parable in Luke 18. The writer provides the interpretive key to the parable's thrust: "To some who were confident of their own righteousness and looked down on everybody else . . ." (v. 9). Luke directly connects self-righteousness with judgmentalism. Where you find one, you will find the other. Self-righteousness breeds judgmentalism. Thinking I'm better than you and looking down on you are two sides of the same coin. Jesus then tells the story:

> Two men went up to the temple to pray, one a Pharisee and the other a tax collector. The Pharisee stood up and prayed about himself: "God, I thank you that I am not like other men—robbers, evildoers, adulterers—or even like this tax collector. I fast twice a week and give a tenth of all I get."
>
> But the tax collector stood at a distance. He would not even look up to heaven, but beat his breast and said, "God, have mercy on me, a sinner."
>
> I tell you that this man, rather than the other, went home justified before God. For everyone who exalts himself will be humbled, and he who humbles himself will be exalted. (Luke 18:10–14)

Notice that the contrast between the two men lies ultimately not in the presence or absence of sin but in their willingness or unwillingness to humbly own and contritely confess it before God. In fact, as others have observed from this parable, the only thing worse than being a robber, evildoer, or adulterer is being proud that you are not one!

While personal peacemaking demands self-examination, true humility goes one step deeper. In his insightful book on Christian marriage, *When Sinners Say "I Do,"* Dave Harvey recommends that before we inspect ourselves, we should *suspect* ourselves.[4] Instead of coming to tense relationships with a presumption of innocence, I should assume in a relational conflict that I likely sinned in some way. (And if I'm later proved wrong, that's fine.) With an assumption of probable guilt, I am more apt to vigorously examine myself. This does not mean that I am

---

[4]Dave Harvey, *When Sinners Say "I Do": Discovering the Power of the Gospel for Marriage* (Wapwallopen, PA: Shepherd, 2007), 63–65.

the only or primary contributor to a conflict; it does mean that I have likely contributed to the problem, and I need to see how.

3. *Jesus assigns a greater weight to your sins than to the other person's sins by calling yours "planks" and his "specks."* As we saw above, the order here is crucial. You must start with you. But the relative weight is no less crucial: your sins are planks; his sins are specks.

Of course, this is relative—his sins may actually be more severe. However, we must *look upon* our offenses as more serious, viewing ours as *major* ("planks") and his as *minor* ("specks"). Even if our offenses may be objectively less serious, Jesus calls us to weigh them as more serious: they are planks, not specks.

This issue of relative weight is critical to grasping Jesus's point. He is speaking to a group of people, not to an individual. It is logically impossible to tell an entire group of people that one listener's sins are somehow objectively worse than the sins of the person next to him, since that other person is also a listener! Two people can't both be worse than each other, but each person can decide to weigh his sin as worse and therefore give greater attention to it.

Suppose I say an unkind word to my friend Mark and he responds by hitting me in the head with a chair, knocking me unconscious. Witnesses phone 911 for help. The police haul Mark in one direction; the paramedics haul me in the other. I wake up the next morning in a hospital bed. What do I report to my friends who visit me? With a bandaged mouth I might mutter some expletives about how Mark mistreated me. I might be quick to report his actions to any who would listen. I might even solicit support from others to side with my view that Mark is a worse sinner than I. After all, isn't that obvious?

However, for me to draw that conclusion would miss Jesus's point. I must look at my sin as serious (a plank) and Mark's as minor (a speck). When I do, this conclusion emerges: "I can't believe I spoke that way to Mark. I was wrong to stab him with my reckless words" (see Prov. 12:18). Objectively, of course, someone could argue that *his* sin was worse than mine. Isn't his violent action unlawful (assault and battery?) in a way that my unkind words are not? Ah, but before you answer yes, ask yourself whose law you are using. While unkind words may not violate civil statutes, they violate God's law. "With the tongue we praise our Lord and Father, and with it we curse men, who have been made in God's likeness. Out of the same mouth come praise and cursing. My brothers, this should not be" (James 3:9–10).

Therefore, I believe that God would want me to contact Mark immediately and seek his forgiveness for my ungodly speech. (After that, if he remained unrepentant, in that same conversation or maybe a later one I could broach the subject of his violent response.) Only by owning 100 percent responsibility for my sin—even if I (arrogantly) think my sin is comparatively only 1 percent of the conflict—will I deal properly with my planks in God-pleasing ways. I must give 100 percent attention to my 1 percent contribution.

While all of us need this insight, it is especially vital for church leaders. The Bible holds leaders to high standards. In my church-conflict intervention ministry I often find that pastors, even if sincerely contrite about their planks, do not confess their sins clearly and thoroughly. Since 1 Timothy 3 and Titus 1 require blameless conduct from pastors, our confessions—the way we handle our own sins—ought to reflect a similar level of blamelessness.

4. At the same time, humbly dealing with your own planks first puts you in a better position to minister to the other person and to help him deal with his sin. Matthew 7:5 ends by giving the purpose for confessing planks. Jesus calls you to deal with your own planks first, "then you will see clearly to remove the speck from your brother's eye." In other words, confession does not stop with helping you but serves also to help the other person.

How does this work? How will humbly confessing my sin help the other person? Let me suggest three ways:

- My confession models humility and may encourage him to do the same. Humility begets humility.
- My confession may lessen his defensiveness. When I own my sin and cease to blame others, I chip away at the defensive wall he has erected.
- My confession may remove the thing that provoked his sin in the first place. When I confess my sin, I deal with what offended the other person.

While at the end of the day these are not the chief reasons to confess our sin—we must do so because our Savior commands us—they add powerful incentive as we pursue relational peace.

How to Confess Your Behavioral Sins

In light of our Lord's command, how should we confess our planks to him and to others we have wronged? Once we see our sinful offenses, how should we make them right? Let's walk through three steps—the first two here, and the third in our next chapter.

Step 1: Identify Your Offenses

The starting place to confess sins is to identify them. I recommend using a written "plank list," a list of your behavioral sins toward the other person.[5] I suggest the list be for your eyes only, as well as anyone who might provide counsel or accountability—a pastor, counselor, or mature Christian friend—but not handed to the offended person. The list should be thorough but not exhaustive. (It is possible to spend too much time in detailed self-examination and thereby delay the next steps.) In other words, it need not address every relational failure—just the main ones, especially those that currently separate you from the other person. Your goal is to clear your conscience, make things right with the other person, and provide an improved relational atmosphere within which to address further problems.

As we approach this task, we must recognize the deceitful power of our remaining sin. The prophet Jeremiah declares,

> The heart is deceitful above all things
>   and beyond cure. (Jer. 17:9a)

The apostle Paul reminds us, "You were taught, with regard to your former way of life, to put off your old self, which is being corrupted by

---

[5]Note that this is a list of *our* sins—the planks in *our* eye—not the other person's sins. I discourage sinned-against people from listing the offender's sins, even for the purpose of handing them over to God, forgiving and praying for the offender, etc. Writing down someone else's sins unwisely focuses on them and embeds them more firmly in my mind. To not record someone's sins (Ps. 130:3–4; 1 Cor. 13:5) seems the wiser course. In chap. 9 we will address how to deal with our memories of the sins of others.

its deceitful desires" (Eph. 4:22). Moreover, Hebrews 3:12–13 warns us, "See to it, brothers, that none of you has a sinful, unbelieving heart that turns away from the living God. But encourage one another daily . . . so that none of you may be hardened by sin's deceitfulness." Beyond the sins we see, there are sins we don't.

Who can understand the deceitful heart? Jeremiah answers:

> I the LORD search the heart
>> and examine the mind,
> to reward a man according to his conduct,
>> according to what his deeds deserve. (Jer. 17:10)

God knows our sins thoroughly, even more than we do. This combination of our self-deception and God's comprehensive knowledge requires us to pray. That is why the psalmist seeks God's forgiveness for both his known and his unknown sins.

> Who can discern his errors?
>> Forgive my hidden faults. (Ps. 19:12)

In Psalm 139 David praises God for his all-seeing, all-knowing, ever-present care. He then closes the psalm with this earnest prayer:

> Search me, O God, and know my heart;
>> test me and know my anxious thoughts.
> See if there is any offensive way in me,
>> and lead me in the way everlasting. (vv. 23–24)

David knows he is a sinner in thought and deed, but he also knows that he may be self-deceived. So he asks his God—the one who searches and knows him thoroughly and intimately (v. 1)—to bring to light his hidden transgressions.

As I worked on the last stages of this book, God gave me a fresh opportunity to apply this truth. A conflict arose between a friend and me. While I sensed I had done something wrong, I wasn't sure what. Even a lengthy conversation didn't illuminate the matter for me. But after a few days of prayerful reflection about my heart attitudes and my specific behavior—asking God to search me and test me—God showed me two specific ways I had failed my friend. I was able to go to him, confess my plank sins, and seek his forgiveness.

How then do we develop such a plank list? Ask God to reveal any ways—even hidden ways—you might have sinned against the other person. If the starting place for confessing sins is identifying them, then the starting place for identifying them is asking God to reveal them. Record what God has brought to your conscience. What do you think you did or said that is wrong, or failed to say or do? What sins has God's Spirit already convicted you of? Consider the "Plank" Commission-Omission Assessment chart above (fig. 4) a useful tool for your self-examination.

In addition, studying the Scriptures will clarify your planks. James 1 provides a powerful image of the Bible as a mirror to show us our sin: "Anyone who listens to the word but does not do what it says is like a man who looks at his face in a mirror and, after looking at himself, goes away and immediately forgets what he looks like" (James 1:23–24). We must learn increasingly to identify our sinful words and actions—omissions and commissions—in light of Scripture.

Furthermore, in cases of more serious sin, it is best to have your pastor, counselor, or accountability partner review your list before you approach the other person. Others can see what we might miss.

Step 2: Confess Your Sins to God, Receive His Forgiveness, and Seek His Help

Always begin with God. All sin is always against God, even if it is also against another human being. In other words, all horizontal sins are also vertical sins. Violations of our Lord Jesus's second great commandment (love your neighbor) also violate the first great commandment (love God).

King David understood this in Psalm 51, his famous confessional psalm linked historically to his adultery with Bathsheba.

> For I know my transgressions,
> and my sin is always before me.
> Against you, you only, have I sinned
> and done what is evil in your sight,
> so that you are proved right when you speak
> and justified when you judge. (vv. 3–4)

David declares that his sin is against God and God only.

Does that language surprise you? I am tempted to object: "Whoa, David, hang on a minute. Against God *only*? What about Bathsheba? You seduced her. What about her husband Uriah? You engineered his death on the front lines of battle. What about the nation? You were God's anointed king but you sinned, deceived the nation, and covered up your sin." How do we explain David's "against you, you only" language? The best answer is that David had such a high view of God and such an intimate relationship with him that it is *as if* God were the only one sinned against. I doubt that David would have denied that he sinned against Bathsheba, Uriah, and the nation. But the primacy of his relationship with his God relativizes all other relationships and explains his "against you, you only" confession.

David is not alone in this perspective. Consider Joseph's God-centered rationale for refusing the sexual advances of Potiphar's wife: "How then could I do such a wicked thing and sin against God?" (Gen. 39:9). Luke 15:18 records the prodigal son's planned confession as both vertical and horizontal: "Father, I have sinned against heaven [an ancient Jewish way to refer to God] and against you [his earthly father]." The gravity of this young man's sin seems to lie not in what he did but against whom he did it. Or listen to the dramatic voice of the exalted Jesus from heaven interrupting Saul of Tarsus in his agenda of persecuting Christians: "Saul, Saul, why do you persecute me?" (Acts 9:4). The Lord views sins against his people as sins against him.

Each month in the small church that I pastored we enjoyed an all-church potluck lunch in our gym. It was a time of relaxation together, delicious food, and rich conversation, as well as an opportunity to connect with visitors. But it was also a prime time for the children to play together. Sometimes an argument would develop that would turn into a fight. Jimmy would hit Joey. If Jimmy's parents saw it, they might walk over to Jimmy, get his attention, and then counsel their son: "Jimmy, hitting Joey was wrong. Tell Joey that you are sorry." And Jimmy would sob his way through a confession to his buddy, and then all would be well (until their next altercation).

There is much to commend in this parental counsel. For parents to even arrive on site to intervene is a good sign; many parents ignore these situations. And guiding children to reconcile with their friends is desperately needed.

But there is something missing here. In fact, it is Someone: God. The above approach ignores the vertical dimension. In these settings, when we merely connect our children to each other, we miss the golden opportunity to connect them first to the Lord, to make things right with him. Instead, parents should wisely seize such an opportunity to point their children to Jesus. Only after Jimmy talks to God to make things right with him should we lead him to make things right with Joey.

Dealing with our own planks in relational conflicts involves this one-two, vertical-horizontal process. This was the apostle Paul's conviction in Acts 24:16: "So I strive always to keep my conscience clear before God and man." Paul understood that being right both with God and with others was his high duty. A clear conscience demanded both vertical and horizontal dimensions.[6]

Furthermore, in confessing our sins to God, it is vital that we view each sin as *sin*, not merely an indiscretion, a failure, a mistake, or a "my bad." One helpful Bible study growth assignment to help us feel the weight of our sin is to look carefully at Ezra 9, Nehemiah 9, and Daniel 9 (END9 is a memory aid)—three Bible chapters that feature God's people confessing their sin in language that reflects its seriousness. These biblical words of confession can help us voice and frame our own confession in a godly way. Their honesty and depth can both startle us and sober us in our honest, heart-searching dealings with our Lord.

What, then, does God want you to do with your plank list? Go to him in prayer to confess your sins, to receive his pardon in Christ, and to seek his help to change. Let the psalms guide you.

> Then I acknowledged my sin to you
> and did not cover up my iniquity.

---

[6]Paul highly valued keeping his conscience clear: "My brothers, I have fulfilled my duty to God in all good conscience to this day" (Acts 23:1b); "My conscience is clear" (1 Cor. 4:4); "Now this is our boast: Our conscience testifies that we have conducted ourselves in the world, and especially in our relations with you, in the holiness and sincerity that are from God. We have done so not according to worldly wisdom but according to God's grace" (2 Cor. 1:12); "I thank God, whom I serve, as my forefathers did, with a clear conscience" (2 Tim. 1:3).

I said, "I will confess
    my transgressions to the LORD"—
and you forgave
    the guilt of my sin. (Ps. 32:5)

I said, "O LORD, have mercy on me;
    heal me, for I have sinned against you." (Ps. 41:4)

Have mercy on me, O God,
    according to your unfailing love;
according to your great compassion
    blot out my transgressions.
Wash away all my iniquity
    and cleanse me from my sin. (Ps. 51:1–2)

We can also rest in the promise of the apostle John, "If we confess our sins, he is faithful and just and will forgive us our sins and purify us from all unrighteousness" (1 John 1:9).

Finally, along with confessing our sin and receiving God's pardon, we should ask the Lord to help us grow and change in whatever specific sin areas we are confessing. In other words, when we come to God, we should seek not only his forgiving mercy but also his empowering grace—"grace to help us in our time of need" (Heb. 4:16) and the power of the Spirit to "put to death the misdeeds of the body" (Rom. 8:13). Here, the classic Bible passages on progressive sanctification will help us (e.g., Romans 6; Gal. 5:16–26; Ephesians 4; 2 Pet. 1:3–9), along with the means of grace God has given us for our growth: both the private avenues (reading, studying, and meditating on Scripture; and prayer) and the corporate avenues (worship, preaching and teaching, prayer, fellowship, baptism, the Lord's Supper, etc.).

Conclusion

In our next chapter we will unfold the third step of confession, the step of humbly going to the other person to confess our sin and seek his forgiveness. But the prerequisite for this, as we have seen in this chapter, is ruthlessly seeing and owning our own sins, confessing them before God, believing the gospel promises of God's forgiveness in Jesus, and depending on his Spirit's help to grow and change. We must not proceed with Step 3 until we reconcile vertically with the Lord.

FOR PERSONAL REFLECTION OR GROUP DISCUSSION

1. What makes it hard for you to *see* the sinful contribution you might have made to a relational conflict? What biblical truths in this chapter can help you examine and own your relational sins?

2. What makes it hard for you to go to God in prayer to confess your sins and to believe that he will forgive you?

3. How have you previously handled situations in which you sensed there was a relational problem but you were not sure that you had done something wrong? Perhaps you have a situation like this right now. How would God want you to handle it better this time or the next time?

6

Apologizing That Makes a Difference

Confessing Our Sins to Those We Have Offended

Why do you look at the speck of sawdust in your brother's eye . . . ?
You hypocrite, first take the plank out of your own eye.
Jesus in Matthew 7:3–5

Well, I'm not gonna apologize if that's what you mean.
Sheriff John T. Chance (John Wayne) after wrongly accusing Feathers
of card cheating in Howard Hawks's film, *Rio Bravo*

So I strive always to keep my conscience clear before God and man.
The apostle Paul in Acts 24:16

There are wise and unwise ways to apologize. One of my favorite bad examples is the humorous greeting card I picked up at a card store. The front had the words "I'm so sorry, but" printed boldly across the top. Below that was a list with checkmark boxes:

- ☐ you provoked me.
- ☐ I was drunk.
- ☐ it was actually your fault.
- ☐ I didn't mean it.
- ☐ I was having a bad day.
- ☐ the timing was off.
- ☐ I love you.
- ☐ you're wrong.
- ☐ you're annoying.
- ☐ it was the PMS talking.

☐ you need help.
☐ I just can't help myself.
☐ I had a bad childhood.
☐ the stars were crossed.
☐ Mercury was in retrograde.
☐ I'm an addict.

The bottom of the front read, "Instructions: Check all that apply." Then inside it said, "I hope you'll accept such a sincere apology."[1] Other than Mercury's alignment, I think I've heard variants of each "sorry" excuse in my counseling ministry.

Thankfully, there are better ways to reconcile with those we have hurt. In our previous chapter we began to unpack the process of making things right with God and with others when we face conflict. Based on our Lord's words in Matthew 7:3–5, we saw the importance of focusing on our contribution to conflict before looking at the other person. We then summarized the first two steps in our three-step process of behavioral level repentance:

- Step 1: Identify your offenses, using a "plank list."
- Step 2: Confess your sins to God, receive his forgiveness, and seek his help.

In this chapter we will focus on the third step, the horizontal step. But first we must address a nagging question we frequently face in relational conflict.

What If I'm Not Sure?

So far we have made a major assumption, namely, that our prayerful, biblical self-examination has revealed "plank" sins against God and others. But there may be times when we honestly do not know whether or how we might have offended someone. Perhaps we feel some distance or tension or coldness from the other person, but we cannot pinpoint our failure. Our plank list is essentially blank.

---

[1]Card by Knock Knock, © Who's There, Inc., www.knockknock.biz.

What should we do if our conscience is clear, yet we still sense relational distance, tension, or estrangement with the other person? We obviously should not confess to something we didn't do merely to appease the other person. Let me suggest two further steps.

First, seek third-party counsel. Ask your pastor, church leader, counselor, or mature Christian friend to help you see your blind spots. He (or she or they) must demonstrate biblical wisdom and confidentiality and must love you enough to be brutally honest with you. In other words, we need people who display Proverbs 27:5–6.

> Better is open rebuke
> than hidden love.
> Wounds from a friend can be trusted,
> but an enemy multiplies kisses.

This third party might also advise you on when and how to approach the other person. In some cases you need not, and should not, divulge the other person's identity: "Pastor, I'm struggling with a relationship with someone and I'd rather not mention his name. I want to do what God wants me to do based on Jesus's words in Matthew 7, but I need to look at the planks in my eye first. Would you be willing to help me see some ways that I might have sinned by omission or commission?"

Second, if you still remain unsure of your planks, then humbly approach the other person to ask him how you might have offended him. But this step applies only when you are *unaware* of any offense you have committed. If you are aware of some planks, deal with those planks by following the process below and in the next chapter. (After you make those offenses right with God and the other person, then you can humbly ask whether there are *other* offenses you have committed.)

Such a humble approach might sound like this: "John, lately I have felt some distance from you, and I'm concerned. There seems to be some relational tension. I wonder if I might have offended you in some way. Have I? I would like to know so I can try to make it right with

---

The Path for Pursuing Peace

Step 1. Please God
Step 2. Repent
  A. Heart sins (beliefs, motives)
  B. Behavior sins (words, actions) (continued)
Step 3. Love the person

you." Then listen carefully and compassionately to his response and any concerns he raises. If he raises a concern, thank him for telling you. If it's obvious that you have sinned, then seek God's forgiveness and John's forgiveness. If not, tell John that you would like to take some time to process his remarks and evaluate your behavior: "Thank you for sharing this. Let me think and pray about what you are saying and get back to you."

Remember that not every offense perceived by another person means that we have sinned. Just because someone feels offended does not mean that I have sinned against him, anymore than the Pharisees' being offended by Jesus meant that Jesus had sinned against them. Therefore, it is best to evaluate the person's concerns in prayer before the Lord prior to our response, lest we offer some on-the-spot confession to simply appease the person or satisfy our confused conscience. Then, be sure to get back to the person.

What If Someone Has Something against Me?

There is one more situation to consider—a variant of the above. What should we do if we learn somehow—from that person or a third party—that someone has something against us? Jesus addresses this matter in Matthew 5:23–24: "Therefore, if you are offering your gift at the altar and there remember that your brother has something against you, leave your gift there in front of the altar. First go and be reconciled to your brother; then come and offer your gift."

Let me draw two insights from this passage. First, Jesus stresses the high priority of relational reconciliation over other acts of worship. Notice the "First . . . then" order in verse 24. Before offering our gift to God, we must make things right with others.

Second, Jesus permits no limitations. He envisions a situation in which you learn that someone "has something against you." He does not say, "Go only if your brother has something *big* against you," as if only major issues matter. I cannot say, "Well, I know Joe has something against me, but it's only a little thing; it will pass and he will forget about it." Issues that seem minor to us might not be minor to the other person. If there is something that divides me from my brother, albeit small in my mind, I still must deal with it.

Jesus also does not say, "Go only if your brother has something *justifiable* against you." I cannot say, "Well, I know Joe has something against me, but he is wrong about that. He has no right to be upset." You and I are not the infallible judges here. We are prone to self-deception, and we need to hear the other person's concerns.

Finally, Jesus does not say, "Go only if your brother has something against you *and you know exactly what it is.*" Jesus does not require that we know what the other person's grievance is before we go. In one case I talked separately to two men at odds with each other. Rich was offended by something Todd did, and he sought my counsel. Since it was a significant matter, I encouraged Rich to call Todd to arrange a sit-down meeting to discuss it privately, per Matthew 18:15. Unaware of my conversation with Rich, Todd concurrently sought my counsel: "Pastor, can you give me some advice? Rich wants to talk with me about something that is bothering him but he wouldn't say what it was. I asked him twice on the phone, but he said that he would rather wait until we sit down to address it. I told Rich that I'd like to know the topic before I agreed to meet. Pastor, what should I do?" I asked him, "Todd, let's look at Matthew 5:23–24 (which we then read). Based on what Jesus says, what do you think Jesus would want you to do?"

After we interacted, I gave him this counsel, "Todd, Jesus is very concerned about your relationship with Rich. He even prioritizes it over various acts of worship. There may be good reasons why Rich did not want to mention the topic over the phone. But Jesus doesn't say that you need to know what the grievance is. He only says that if you are aware Rich has something against you—and you are aware—then you should talk to Rich. So I recommend that you call him today, schedule a time to meet with him, and go armed with the strength of Jesus and his Spirit to humbly address whatever Rich brings up." I later learned that they resolved it well.

Step 3: Confess Your Sins to the Other Person, and Seek His Forgiveness

Having sought and received God's vertical forgiveness through Jesus Christ, we must now approach the other person we have offended to seek horizontal forgiveness from him. What does a good confession look like? How do we offer an apology that makes a difference—an apology that reflects the depth and breadth of our sin and demonstrates to the other person both our remorse for hurting him and our desire to receive his forgiveness?

Among the many valuable resources developed by Ken Sande and Peacemaker Ministries is the "Seven A's of Confession."[2] Each one reflects wisdom; together they form seven vital characteristics of an effective confession. In the following pages I will provide my own summary and application of each of Sande's seven headings.

1. Address everyone involved. As we saw in chapter 5, the first person we must always address is God. The second person(s) must be the other party or parties we sinned against directly. But in some cases, after making things right with God and the person we offended, we should include others as a subsequent step. Like who? Here the old adage holds: The circle of confession must be as big as the circle of offense. In other words, if I sinned against one person, I need to seek forgiveness from one person. If I sinned against six people, I need to seek forgiveness from six people. If I sinned against two hundred people . . . And so on.

One category to consider is those who witnessed the offense. In one conflicted church my conciliation team met with a church leader who had sinned against his pastor several years before by unjustly calling him a heretic. Such a serious charge led to an immediate breach in their relationship. Thankfully, the church leader later repented. He met with the pastor and sought his forgiveness, and the two were reconciled. But that was not the whole story. The accusation was serious; what made it worse was that he made that charge in the presence of over a dozen other church leaders. Based on this first *A*, the church leader realized that it was not enough to gain the pastor's forgiveness. So he sought out each fellow leader who had been present when he made his false charge. In some cases that meant personal phone calls or visits, even to those who had left the church or relocated. In each case he confessed his sin, reported that he had sought and received the pastor's forgiveness, and sought and received their forgiveness as well.

---

[2]Excerpted from Ken Sande, *The Peacemaker: A Biblical Guide to Resolving Personal Conflict*, 3rd ed. (Grand Rapids: Baker, 2004), chap. 6. Used by permission from Peacemaker Ministries. www.Peacemaker.net. The Seven A's are also found in Ken Sande, with Tom Raabe, *Peacemaking for Families: A Biblical Guide to Managing Conflict in Your Home* (Wheaton, IL: Tyndale, 2002), chap. 4, and other resources from Peacemaker Ministries.

Another category is those who suffer because of your sin. This might include the spouse or family members of the person you offended. If you sinned against your own spouse, then confessing to your children or even to your in-laws might be proper. If you are a leader—especially if your sin has resulted in termination, resignation, or public disgrace—then confessing to your entire organization, church, or company would often be proper, depending on the offense. Aside from making things right with these other individuals affected by your sin, such confession communicates to the other party that you value his reputation and that you are willing to go the extra mile to make things right in every way. It also models for the onlookers how followers of Jesus seek to handle their sins in humble ways.

At the same time, this truth has a corollary. While the circle of confession must be as big as the circle of offense, it must be no bigger. We must not broadcast to everyone confessions that should only be made to those we have specifically offended.

2. *Avoid "if," "but," and "maybe."* Perhaps you have been the recipient of such an "if" confession from someone: "I'm sorry if I hurt you." To which we are tempted to respond: "If? What do you mean '*if* you hurt me'? If? Don't you know that you hurt me?" In fact, "if" confessions really say this: "I don't know how I hurt you, and I really don't care to know. And since I don't know what I did, I will probably do it again. But if you are going to be so whiny and hypersensitive that we can't go forward in our relationship until I say 'I'm sorry,' then, well, I'm sorry. Okay?" But true confessions allow no doubt or shade. You must take full responsibility for your own sin.

In a similar way, "but" confessions also fail to accept full responsibility. "I'm sorry I am late getting home from work," a husband tells his wife, "but if you had called to remind me, I would have been here on time." "I am sorry I yelled at you, son, but if you took the trash out when you were supposed to do so, I would not have." The insertion of a "but" virtually negates the confession. It is like placing your cursor in the middle of the above sentences, highlighting the first half (the confessional part), and then hitting the delete key. "But" apologies shift blame; they declare that our failures are not fully our fault.

One step to help detect and expose the "if" and "but" components in our confessions is to write them out. When I coach someone in conflict who needs to make a confession, I typically teach him the truths of Matthew 7 above (and other passages), assign him to draft a plank list, and then meet with him to discuss his planks and to help him craft his confession. More than one draft is sometimes needed to eliminate any "if," "but," or similar contaminants.

3. *Admit specifically.* One of the best ways to increase the effectiveness of a sin confession is to be specific. Whatever sincerity drives it, an "I'm sorry, son, that I've been a lousy dad" confession remains weak. How have you failed as father? In what ways? People sin in the concrete, not the abstract. Not only does a specific confession show thoughtfulness, sincerity, and sorrow; it also sets a specific agenda for change. A careful study of Scripture will help us clarify the concrete ways we have sinned against the other person in word and action, by commission and omission. A good confession will admit that I have been a lousy dad because I have done or said A, B, and C and failed to do or say X, Y, and Z.

4. *Acknowledge the hurt.* This frequently overlooked fourth *A* carries powerful potential to reconcile relationships. Acknowledging the hurt means expressing sorrow for the way our sin has made life hard for the other person. How has our sin embarrassed, inconvenienced, tempted, injured, or provoked him?

True repentance always carries some sense of remorse. On some level I feel bad about what I have done. Concern for the offended party is in view. I am sorry for my sin not because I was caught and will face bad consequences but because of what it did to God and to the other person. If my only sorrow lies in the consequences of getting caught, I will simply seek to be more shrewd and sneaky the next time I want to sin. In true repentance I realize I have grieved God's Spirit (Eph. 4:30) and hurt, offended, or embarrassed someone else.

As we saw previously, this does not mean that my sin somehow *caused* someone's sinful reaction. People are not machines. I cannot take responsibility for the other person's wrong response to me. Jesus was not responsible for his disciples' doubts when they woke him during a severe storm and questioned whether he cared for them (Mark 4). Jesus was not responsible for Mary and Martha's unbelief when they expressed their irritation that Jesus did not race to their brother's deathbed and prevent him from dying (John 11). Though Jesus was sinless and we are not, our wrong actions do not cause other people to sin in return.

Nevertheless, our sins do genuinely affect people by hurting them, and a wise confession seeks to feel that hurt and convey that regret. What does a confession that acknowledges the hurt look like? Suppose my wife and I dine with another couple at a restaurant, and in the course of conversation I say something unkind about Lauren. On our way home God's Spirit convicts me of my sin. There are two possible ways for me to apologize to her (after first quietly making things right with God):

> Good Confession: "I'm sorry, Lauren, for what I said to our friends. I was wrong. Will you please forgive me?"

That's a good confession, and as professor I would give it a *B* grade. But here's a better one:

> Better Confession: "I'm sorry, Lauren, for what I said to our friends. I was wrong. And I know I hurt you and embarrassed you in front of our friends. Will you please forgive me?"

That confession earns an *A*. Why? Because it acknowledges the *impact* that my sin had on the other person. The confession itself is an act of love designed to show my wife my care for her, not merely my desire to clear my own conscience. (Of course, in keeping with my above commitment to address everyone involved, I would also want to contact the other couple and confess this sin to them.) Or consider some more examples of confessions that acknowledge the hurt:

- "I am sorry that I said those critical things about you in the church parking lot and cut you down in front of our friends; that must have hurt."
- "I got your phone message asking me to send you the report you wanted. I am sorry that I failed to send it to you and I left you without the support and information you needed for your meeting."

- "I am sorry that I lied to you. I know that is going to make it much harder for you to trust me next time."

At the same time, when you seek to acknowledge the impact of your sin, realize that the other person might be reluctant to admit his hurts, for various reasons. How should you respond if the person replies to your confession with a simple, "Oh, it was nothing"? If your offense was not major, then you can say, "Thank you," and move forward with the relationship. But in cases of more serious sin, or if the person might be minimizing your offense or hiding his hurt, it may be best to try to draw him out gently: "Well, I really appreciate your graciousness in calling it 'nothing,' but I really hurt you (or embarrassed you or inconvenienced you), and I want you to know that I am grieved by that." Or, "Well, I appreciate your graciousness in calling it 'nothing,' but I know that if I were in your shoes, I might have trouble letting it go." (At this point, you might even share how you have been sinned against in a similar way.) Whatever the method, inviting discussion shows the depth of your own repentance and may help the person address some unresolved feelings. Inviting and encouraging the person to talk about it—without pressuring or insisting—shows that you care for the one you have hurt.

5. Accept consequences. The biblical truth underlying this component of a godly confession is that we should bring forth fruit in keeping with our repentance. Let me suggest three categories of consequences.

First, our confession and repentance may require some form of restitution or justice. That might include financial reparations (Ex. 21:18–35; 22:1–15; Lev. 6:1–5; Num. 5:5–10; Deut. 22:8; Luke 19:8–9) or other forms of justice, especially for criminal actions. As Proverbs 19:19 observes,

> A hot-tempered man must pay the penalty;
> if you rescue him, you will have to do it again.

True repentance may require the repentant one to suffer the just consequences of his wrong choices. The repentant thief who hung on the cross next to Jesus still died. If I borrow your book and tear some pages, I should buy you a new copy. If I forget to pick up a gallon of milk on the way home from work, then I need to go out to the store to buy one.

Second, a godly confession might entail a loss of privileges or possessions. If I borrow your book and tear some pages, I may lose my borrowing privileges, even if I buy you a replacement. In the Luke 15 story of the welcoming father, the prodigal son humbled himself and offered to relinquish his sonship status: "I am no longer worthy to be called your son; make me like one of your hired men" (Luke 15:19). And in 2 Samuel 12, while King David received God's forgiveness, the severity of his sin resulted in the death of his newborn son: "Then David said to Nathan, 'I have sinned against the LORD.' Nathan replied, 'The LORD has taken away your sin. You are not going to die. But because by doing this you have made the enemies of the LORD show utter contempt, the son born to you will die'" (vv. 13–14).

Third, and most commonly, the other person may be slow or even unwilling to forgive us or to trust us. In other words, even if I sincerely repent, there is no guarantee that the person will forgive me or trust me. While he may choose to be merciful, we must relinquish any presumed right to be forgiven. Proverbs 18:19 reminds us,

> An offended brother is more unyielding than a fortified city,
>   and disputes are like the barred gates of a citadel.

I infer from this that it would be easier for me to march downtown and take over the capital city of my state than to reconcile a relationship with someone I have offended. It would be easier for me to penetrate a barred fortress than to resolve conflicts with some individuals.

We see this dynamic sometimes in cases of adultery.[3] A husband commits sexual infidelity. He sincerely repents and seeks his wife's forgiveness. In some cases she decides not to forgive him. In other cases she grants him forgiveness, and they begin to rebuild their relationship. Occasionally, however, another dynamic emerges. The wife forgives. But one day, perhaps two months later, the husband comes home from work three hours late. She asks him—perhaps innocently

---

[3]For an application of the truths in this chapter to those rocked by adultery or other serious betrayal, see Robert D. Jones, *Restoring Your Broken Marriage: Healing after Adultery* (Greensboro, NC: New Growth, 2009).

and caringly, perhaps suspiciously and anxiously (after all, he has lied before)—a simple question: "Honey, where were you?" But instead of answering her question, he explodes with anger: "Why are you asking me that? I thought you forgave me! Don't you trust me?" And the tensions mount.

What should this couple do? The husband needs to recognize that even though he has repented, one consequence of his betrayal is that his wife might struggle with doubts. Of course, depending on the motive behind her question, she might need to address any of her lingering fears or resentment. But the husband must deal biblically with his anger. Inquiries about his whereabouts are consequences he must patiently accept.

Why is it important that we accept the consequences? For one thing, it demonstrates our sincerity and shows the offended person that we are not asking for forgiveness merely to avoid consequences. By my willingness to accept consequences that are just, even painful, I show true contrition. In addition, it lessens the likelihood of our repeating the same sin. Recall Proverbs 19:19 above.

> A hot-tempered man must pay the penalty;
> if you rescue him, you will have to do it again.

Having to confess the same sin each time, and bearing the appropriate consequences, should deter us from repeating the same offense.

We need to insert one more qualification about accepting consequences: do not confuse punishment with consequences. "Therefore, there is now no condemnation for those who are in Christ Jesus" (Rom. 8:1). As Christians we must remember that God *punished Jesus* as the substitute for our sin.

> He who did not spare his own Son, but gave him up for us all—how will he not also, along with him, graciously give us all things? Who will bring any charge against those whom God has chosen? It is God who justifies. Who is he that condemns? Christ Jesus, who died—more than that, who was raised to life—is at the right hand of God and is also interceding for us. (Rom. 8:32–34)

101

He himself bore our sins in his body on the tree. . . . For Christ died for sins once for all, the righteous for the unrighteous, to bring you to God. (1 Pet. 2:24; 3:18)

Because of the cross God does not hold the believer's sins against him. If God truly wanted to *punish* us, each of us would be condemned to hell, and Jesus would not have died.

6. *Alter your behavior (or at least explain how you intend to do so).* Accepting consequences reflects the passive side of showing the fruit of repentance. The active side involves developing, voicing, and carrying out a plan to change our behavior. Proverbs 28:13 sets the standard.

> He who conceals his sins does not prosper,
>> but whoever confesses and renounces them finds mercy.

Perhaps the change is simple and the alteration can be made immediately: a decision can be made or unmade today; a phone call or visit can be accomplished tonight; an activity can be stopped this moment. But perhaps it is complex and will require more time: patterns of anger, sexual lust, and sinful speech will require an ongoing plan for progressive sanctification.

And so the question we must ask, especially when addressing serious sins or patterns of sin, is twofold: Do we have a practical plan to avoid recurrence? And can we state it? I recommend a written plan to best allow careful thinking, ongoing editing, and sharing with accountability partners. The plan should address what, when, how, and with whom we will pursue changes. (For example: "The next time I am tempted to gossip, I will seek help from my wife and my pastor or small group leader.") It must be practical. Think of a football team's game plan or a nurse's care plan for patients discharged from a hospital.

How does this increase the effectiveness of our confession? Like the previous *A*'s, it shows the depth of our sorrow and sincerity, it helps us make specific changes, and it invites the offended person, if he truly forgives, to become an ally and help us carry out our growth plan.

7. Ask for forgiveness, and allow time. This last component aims to bring closure to the repentance by encouraging the offended to respond to our confession. "I am sorry for what I did and for how I hurt you. I was wrong. Will you please forgive me?"

Asking does not mean demanding. Remember that the offended partner might be slow to forgive. We must rest in God's decided, declared, and promised forgiveness, even if the other person does not forgive. We should desire his forgiveness; we must never require it.

The above becomes doubly important when the offense has been severe. A good rule of thumb is that the greater the sin, the more time we should allow. In fact, in some cases it might be premature to even ask for forgiveness. A better approach might be: "While I would like you to forgive me—I would greatly treasure that—I also know I hurt you very deeply, and I know it may be hard for you to forgive me after what I've done. I understand that this may be very difficult for you, and it may take time for you to get to that point. That's okay. I understand." (Remember that "an offended brother is more unyielding than a fortified city"—Prov. 18:19.)

There are several hazards to avoid. For one thing, we can become self-righteous and judgmental: "I asked you to forgive me and now, according to the Bible, God says you *must* forgive me. If you refuse to forgive me, then you are a worse sinner than I am. So, do you forgive me?" So sinister is the power of our pride that even a godly act like confessing sin can become an occasion for further sin.

Another problem arises when definitions differ. It is easy for either party to assume he understands what forgiveness is. The repentant person might assume that the relationship is now completely restored, only to find that the person who voices forgiveness still remains distant. The repentant person might wonder whether his confession was sufficient or whether the forgiving person was sincere. In granting forgiveness, the forgiving person might not want a restored relationship. Therefore, it is often wise for the repenting person who receives forgiveness to seek clarification of what the forgiving person means:[4] "Does this mean we can still be friends?" "Can we still work together?" "Will you be able to trust me?"

---

[4]We will address how to forgive someone in chap. 8 below.

Finally, in allowing the other person time, we must not drop our concern or let go of the relationship. The time cannot be unlimited; time does not heal all wounds. A truce, cold war, and distance are not the relational *shalom* that Jesus Christ died and rose to purchase and cultivate in his people. Our goal must always be to please God by pursuing peace. As Romans 12:18 reminds us, "If it is possible, as far as it depends on you, live at peace with everyone." In our last chapter we will address what to do if the other party does not respond to our peacemaking efforts. Below are several initial steps briefly stated.

What If the Person Won't Forgive You?

There is no guarantee that even a perfect confession will compel the other person to forgive. How should we respond if he won't? Let me suggest the following path:

1. Seek counsel from your pastor or a biblical counselor for any or all of the following steps.
2. Allow more time. Do not expect him to forgive you immediately upon your request. Don't despair if he delays. Don't pressure him. Give God time to soften his heart.
3. Pray for him in concentrated ways.
4. Consider making a second or third effort to talk with him.
5. If you are able to converse with him, ask him for any reasons why he will not forgive you, and try to address them wisely, sensitively, calmly, and humbly.
6. Repeat, in different words, the specific seven A's above that he most needs to hear again, and assess what action steps (alter your behavior) need to be taken or improved.
7. Acknowledge that you understand that it may be hard for him to forgive. Remember that one of the consequences you may bear (above) is the other person's slowness to forgive you or trust you.
8. Give him still more time. Do not pressure him. Continue to pray for him.
9. At every point along the path, beware of
   • self-righteous, condescending attitudes,
   • lecturing him,
   • minimizing your sin,
   • bitterness and resentment growing in your heart.
10. Encourage him to talk to a pastor, elder, mature Christian friend, or counselor, or to read a good book or booklet on forgiveness.

11. In some cases, at some point, you may need to confront him about his sin of unforgiveness, and even appeal to him about involving a third-party facilitator to assist you. If the person remains resistant, you may need to bring other believers as witnesses or mediators (Matt. 18:15–17). We will address this in chapter 12.

12. In all this, if you have sought to please the Lord, even if you have done so imperfectly (which is true of all our faith and obedience until he returns), then rejoice in God's favor on you. By faith hear his "well done, good and faithful servant," as your head hits your pillow.

Conclusion

The goal of this chapter has been specific: to help us present an apology that makes a difference in a conflicted relationship. While we cannot control the other person's response, we can wisely and prayerfully frame our words in ways that please God and truly love our neighbor, maximizing the likelihood of genuine reconciliation. In our next chapter we will explore the proper attitudes we need to display as we move toward the other party.

For Personal Reflection or Group Discussion

1. Reflect on the efforts you have made in the past to apologize to those you have wronged, as well as the efforts others have made to make things right with you. Where have you followed the seven A's above (even if you didn't have the list)? Where have you fallen short?

2. Which of the seven A's above do you find hardest to practice? Why? For this specific weakness, consider digging into God's Word on that point, praying specifically for the Spirit's help, and sharing your struggle with a pastor, biblical counselor, or mature Christian friend to seek counsel and accountability.

3. Your friend tells you about some way that his close friend or spouse seriously offended him and that the relationship is now in trouble. Yet, as you listen, you can tell that your friend was not blameless in this. What might you say to help him become willing to look at his planks? How might you then coach him to go to the other person with a seven-A confession?

7

Cultivating Grace Attitudes

Putting on the Clothing of Christ

When Christ rules in the heart, his peace will rule in the fellowship.
Dick Lucas

Because of your great compassion you did not abandon them in the desert.
Nehemiah 9:19

One thing that I least like doing is something that I have to do, and it is something I have to do every day. I hate doing it, and I wish I didn't have to. But it's something I must do. It is getting dressed. If I had my druthers, I would stay in my pajamas or gym shorts all day. I simply do not like changing clothes. What a waste of time and money to shop for clothing, and what a waste of precious morning minutes to put them on (not to mention when my job requires a jacket or tie). But I get dressed each morning because it is right. My friends and neighbors definitely don't want to see me in my pajamas.

However, there's something I like to do even less than *getting* dressed. It's *picking out* which clothes to wear. I hate getting dressed; I really hate choosing what to wear. Thankfully, I have an answer to that problem: God gave me a wife. Lauren likes to help her fashion-challenged husband by laying out clothes for me in the mornings. I am so grateful to have

The Path for Pursuing Peace
Step 1. Please God
Step 2. Repent
Step 3. Love the person
A. Attitudes of Grace
B. Forgive
C. Confront
D. Serve

someone who picks tasteful attire for me. All I have to do is put on the clothes she lovingly provides.

In a similar way, in Colossians 3:12–14 God has laid out for us clothing to wear. In one sense, it's not new—it's new *to us*. In fact, it is used—hand-me-down. It is nothing less than the very attire—the exact outfit—that the Son of God wore on this earth and continues to wear each day. It is the clothing of Jesus, and he gives it to us. He purchased it for us to wear. Moreover, it is clothing that is always fitting in every season, on any occasion.

Colossians 3:12–14

What does this God-given attire look like? Paul unveils the outfit.

> Therefore, as God's chosen people, holy and dearly loved, clothe your-selves with compassion, kindness, humility, gentleness and patience. Bear with each other and forgive whatever grievances you may have against one another. Forgive as the Lord forgave you. And over all these virtues put on love, which binds them all together in perfect unity. (Col. 3:12–14)

We will look at these Christlike attitudes in this chapter. But before we do, let's see their overall connection to peacemaking. Paul continues, "Let the peace of Christ rule in your hearts, since as members of one body you were called to peace" (v. 15). In other words, the peace within the church envisioned in verse 15 flows from the grace attitudes pictured in verses 12–14. But what does the peace in verse 15 involve? Based on the second part of the text, most commentators rightly see this peace as relational and corporate more than internal and individual.[1] As Dick Lucas summarizes:

> This exhortation is sometimes misunderstood as a subjective guide to decision-making. Paul is not speaking here of an inner sense of peace as God's gift to those who are in his will: this would make little sense of

---

[1] For example, see P. T. O'Brien, "Colossians," in D. A. Carson, ed., *New Bible Commentary: 21st Century Edition*, 4th ed. (Downers Grove, IL: InterVarsity, 1994), Col. 3:12–17; James D. G. Dunn, *The Epistles to the Colossians and to Philemon: A Commentary on the Greek Text* (Grand Rapids: Eerdmans, 1996), 233; and N. T. Wright, *Colossians and Philemon: An Introduction and Commentary*, Tyndale New Testament Commentaries (Downers Grove, IL: InterVarsity, 1986), 147–48.

the second half of the sentence which must control the interpretation, especially if this interpretation is to be kept in line with the context.

Instead, the passage is about relational peace within the church.

> It is inconceivable that those who share with one another the benefits of that great peace-making work of the cross (1:20) should live with any hatred or contempt for each other in their hearts. The Christian congregation should be a realm of peace just because every Christian is totally committed to the rule of peace. When Christ rules in the heart, his peace will rule in the fellowship.[2]

The Lord Jesus who purchased and brought us his peace (Col. 1:15–23) now enables and calls us to live out that peace with one another in our local church.

Our Identity in Christ

In this chapter we will examine eight godly attitudes in Colossians 3:12–14 that are foundational to biblical peacemaking. But to understand them we need to understand the preceding context. In Colossians 3:1–4 the apostle reminds believers of their new spiritual position in Christ. We died with him, we were raised with him, and we will gloriously appear with him when he returns. Because we are united to Jesus, we should fix our hearts and minds on him (vv. 1–2) and put off all vestiges of our remaining sin (vv. 5–11). The sins listed are comprehensive, reflecting the attitudes and practices of our old nature. In contrast, Paul calls us to live out the new life that God is forming in us, patterned after Jesus's glorious image.

In verse 12, the apostle cites three identity descriptors that are foundational to the eight peacemaking qualities: we are "God's chosen people, holy and dearly loved."

First, God chose us. Nothing will encourage us more than to know that God has handpicked us, that in eternity past he chose us to be saved through faith in Jesus Christ. Yet nothing will humble us more

---

[2]R. C. Lucas, *Fullness and Freedom: The Message of Colossians and Philemon* (Downers Grove, IL: InterVarsity, 1980), 153–54.

than to know that this was not based on anything good in us, but solely because of his sheer pleasure and unconditional grace.

How does this impact the way we handle conflict? Knowing our secure acceptance by the God of the universe allows us to absorb mistreatment and injustice:

- Who cares if your teacher doesn't like you or if your coworkers criticize you? God has favored you.
- Why does it bother you so much that the band director bypassed you or the coach benched you? Almighty God has chosen you.
- Why are you jealous that your friends are married and you are not, or upset that the spouse you do have mistreats you? Jesus Christ is your life.
- Why does it matter so much that your boss ignores you? Your Lord has promoted you from death to life.
- What about the bitterness you feel after your church bypassed you for that ministry position you wanted? The God of heaven has singled you out for spectacular glory.

Second, God possesses us. The term *holy* (or sanctified) fundamentally involves being possessed by God and set apart for his special purpose.[3] And so "holy" in verse 12, especially when sandwiched between "chosen" and "loved," means that God has made us his. He has set us apart as his possession; we belong to him. Moreover, by his Holy Spirit he desires not merely to own us but to control us (Gal. 5:16–26; Eph. 5:18). When a pro athlete performs at an exceptionally high level, sports announcers say that he is "playing like a man possessed." That's the Christian's unique identity when we face conflict: We belong to God and we handle adversity like men and women possessed by him.

Third, God loves us. The apostle completes his triad of identity descriptors in Colossians 3:12. We are "dearly loved." Through Jesus's death, the Christian knows the everlasting love of God—the love that

[3]See David Peterson, *Possessed by God: A New Testament Theology of Sanctification and Holiness* (Grand Rapids: Eerdmans, 1995), 136–37 (summary); John Murray, *The Collected Writings of John Murray*, vol. 2, *Select Lectures in Systematic Theology* (Carlisle, PA: Banner of Truth, 1977), 277–84; and D. A. Carson, *For the Love of God: A Daily Companion for Discovering the Riches of God's Word*, vol. 1 (Wheaton, IL: Crossway, 1998), August 27 entry.

never ceases, never lets go, and never gives up. Even when people turn against us, God's love remains. Moreover, even when we mess up—when our desires to please God falter—God's love assures us. J. I. Packer writes:

> There is tremendous relief in knowing that His love to me is utterly realistic, based at every point on prior knowledge of the worst about me, so that no discovery now can disillusion him about me, in the way I am so often disillusioned about myself, and quench His determination to bless me. . . . For some unfathomable reason, He wants me as His friend, and desires to be my friend, and has given His Son to die for me in order to realize this purpose.[4]

God loves us even though he knows the very worst about us. He does not love us because we have been good boys and girls or because we are loving, loveable, or lovely. He loves us simply because he wants to love us, for reasons known only to him. The cross is the result of that love.

Grace Attitudes

In Colossians 3:5–11 Paul describes the evil we must put off. Verses 12–14 set forth the eight attitudes we are to put on. The Greek New Testament verb translated "put on" or "clothe yourself with" continues the clothing metaphor begun with the "put off" exhortations in verses 5–11. Paul lays out eight articles of clothing that make up this outfit.

1. Clothe Yourselves with Compassion

Compassion is that inward, deeply felt emotional response of pity for a suffering person, coupled with a desire to alleviate that suffering. Notice three ingredients: compassion (1) sees the suffering person, (2) feels tender pity in response to the suffering, and (3) acts to alleviate that suffering when possible. That sense of tender pity must be distinguished from any self-righteous, condescending, air of superiority that looks down on the sufferer but remains aloof and unengaged. As one commentator notes, "The Christian, then, is to be a man of pity, a man who cannot see suffering or need or distress without a sword of

---

[4]J. I. Packer, *Knowing God* (Downers Grove, IL: InterVarsity, 1973), 37.

grief and pity piercing his own heart. There can be no more complete opposites than callousness and Christianity."[5] Godly compassion feels the needs of others and seeks to help.

We see this in God the Father: "Praise be to the God and Father of our Lord Jesus Christ, the Father of compassion and the God of all comfort, who comforts us in all our troubles, so that we can comfort those in any trouble with the comfort we ourselves have received from God" (2 Cor. 1:3–4). We see this in Jesus as he ministers among the crowds: "Jesus went through all the towns and villages, teaching in their synagogues, preaching the good news of the kingdom and healing every disease and sickness. When he saw the crowds, he had compassion on them, because they were harassed and helpless, like sheep without a shepherd" (Matt. 9:35–36).[6] Jesus *saw* the sufferers (harassed, helpless, shepherd-less sheep), *felt* their need (had compassion), and *acted* to help them (by teaching, preaching, and healing).

Of course, it is one thing to show compassion to victims. But what about those who suffer because of their own sins? The testimony of God's compassion in Nehemiah 9 stuns us.

> But they, our forefathers, became arrogant and stiff-necked, and did not obey your commands. They refused to listen and failed to remember the miracles you performed among them. They became stiff-necked and in their rebellion appointed a leader in order to return to their slavery. But you are a forgiving God, gracious and compassionate, slow to anger and abounding in love. Therefore you did not desert them, even when they cast for themselves an image of a calf and said, "This is your god, who brought you up out of Egypt," or when they committed awful blasphemies.
>
> Because of your great compassion you did not abandon them in the desert. By day the pillar of cloud did not cease to guide them on their path, nor the pillar of fire by night to shine on the way they were to take. You gave your good Spirit to instruct them. You did not withhold your

---

[5] William Barclay, *The All-Sufficient Christ: Studies in Paul's Letter to the Colossians* (Philadelphia: Westminster Press, 1963), 126.

[6] The Gospel writers record six other scenes where the same Greek term is used to show Jesus's compassion for others (Matt. 20:34; Mark 1:41; 6:34; 8:2; 9:22; Luke 7:13); Jesus also attributes compassion to both the loving Samaritan (Luke 10:33) and the prodigal son's waiting father (Luke 15:20).

manna from their mouths, and you gave them water for their thirst.
(Neh. 9:16–20)

Here we see God's amazing grace for people who not only do not deserve
it but have provoked his wrath and deserve the exact opposite. And
what Nehemiah 9 specifies as the attribute that led God to show goodness to rebels and blasphemers is his compassion. This insight is vital
in our conflicts. It is easy to become so bitter over our own hurts that
we cannot see the hurts that the other person experiences. The result
is a relational gridlock. Godlike compassion toward the other party,
however, includes seeing, feeling, and trying to alleviate the suffering
even of those who have mistreated us. Such compassion can begin to
break through the relational impasse.

2. Clothe Yourselves with Kindness

Kindness means showing mercy and doing good even to people who do
not deserve it or who deserve the opposite. The term frequently refers
to the Lord's saving actions (e.g., Eph. 2:7; Titus 3:4). In the same way,
Jesus calls us to be like God the Father, showing kindness even toward
the ungrateful and rebellious: "But love your enemies, do good to them,
and lend to them without expecting to get anything back. Then your
reward will be great, and you will be sons of the Most High, because he
is kind to the ungrateful and wicked. Be merciful, just as your Father
is merciful" (Luke 6:35–36).

God extends his saving kindness even to the undeserving and even
to the counter-deserving. It is one thing to give $300 to a stranger who
deserves nothing from you; it's another thing to give $300 to some-
one who has spit in your face or attacked you and who deserves the
opposite of kindness.

Of course this is not our natural tendency when we face conflict.
Too often our hearts reflect the opposite:

- "That's the last time I do him a favor."
- "Enough is enough. This relationship is over."
- "No one will do that to me again."
- "After all I've done, this is the thanks I get!"

Thankfully, this is not the way God treats us, and it is not the way we have to treat others. How is it possible for you and me to show kindness in these situations? The answer is simple but profound: kindness does not depend on the other person's character; it depends on us. God does not call us to show kindness to the other person because the other person deserves it, but *because God deserves it* and because he wants his sons and daughters to be like him.

3. Clothe Yourselves with Humility

Humility means recognizing that all you have comes from God and that you are absolutely dependent on him as both your Creator and your Redeemer.

Humility was no more valued in Paul's day than it is in our day. Both worlds were, and are, populated by prideful people. People swaggered and strutted, like they do today. They admired dominance, self-assertion, and one-upmanship. Humility in Paul's Roman culture was an abject, servile quality, yet Paul exalts it as a strength in Colossians 3:12, as does the rest of our Bible.

> This is the one I esteem:
> > he who is humble and contrite in spirit,
> > and trembles at my word. (Isa. 66:2)

> He has showed you, O man, what is good.
> > And what does the LORD require of you?
> To act justly and to love mercy
> > and to walk humbly with your God. (Mic. 6:8)

All of you, clothe yourselves with humility toward one another, because,

> "God opposes the proud
> > but gives grace to the humble." (1 Pet. 5:5; also James 4:6)

God dwells with the humble, esteems and highly values the humble, walks with the humble, justifies and exalts the humble, and gives them grace.

What does that look like in our horizontal relationships? Biblical humility involves an utter trust in God that allows others to be honored above me. Humility means preferring others over me. "Do nothing out of selfish ambition or vain conceit, but in humility consider others better than yourselves" (Phil. 2:3). It means taking the last seat as a guest at someone's dinner table, letting another car switch lanes in front of you, and waiting for others to go through the line first at a church potluck meal. Since God is in complete control, I don't have to be first. I can lower myself, let others have the top spot, and know he will provide for me in his way, in his time.

4. Clothe Yourselves with Gentleness

Popular understandings of gentleness sometimes confuse it with weakness or femininity. This is a mistake. The apostle Paul was not a weak man. Yet he describes himself to the Thessalonians as "gentle among you" (1 Thess. 2:7; cf. 2 Cor. 10:1). Jesus was not a weak man. Yet he said of himself, "I am gentle and humble in heart" (Matt. 11:28–29). Someone has observed that this is the only place in the Gospel records where Jesus describes his inner character. As I regularly remind men, if our definition of manhood does not feature humility and gentleness as central, then it is sub-Christian. That lesson doubles for men who are Christian leaders. At his core, the greatest Leader who walked this earth was gentle and humble.

5. Clothe Yourselves with Patience

Several New Testament Greek terms can be translated as "patience." One term connotes endurance under trial and perseverance amid hardship. But Colossians 3:12 uses a different term that primarily concerns *relational* patience—being long-suffering, long-fused, and long-tempered toward those who irritate us. William Barclay describes it as

> the ability to bear with people, not to grow angry or bitter or irritated or annoyed with them, even when they are foolish or ungrateful or even apparently hopeless. . . . It is the ability serenely to take people as they are, with all their faults and all their failings, and with all the ways in which they hurt and wound us, and never stop caring for them and bearing with them.[7]

---

[7]Barclay, *The All-Sufficient Christ*, 123–24.

What does this look like in the daily life of conflict? How well do you show self-restraint toward people who provoke you? Slow people? Boring people? Messy people? Gabby people? Thickheaded people? How about drivers on the road? ("Don't they know I've got to be somewhere!")

6. Clothe Yourselves with Forbearance

Paul continues in verse 13, "Bear with each other and forgive whatever grievances you may have against one another." Forbearance—an older term for bearing with each other—is a synonym for relational patience.

I appreciate the Bible's realism. The apostle assumes that people will annoy us and that relationships become tense. As we saw in chapter 2, conflict is inevitable. Jesus knows that until he returns, there will be problems in his church. He knows that teen communication, or the lack of it, will frustrate parents. He knows that husbands will leave socks on the floor, and wives will want to talk at times when husbands don't. He knows that new church leaders will want to do things differently than previous church leaders. Learning to bear with one another is an indispensable skill for pursuing peace in daily living.

7. Clothe Yourselves with Christlike Forgiveness

Not only will people irk us; they will sin against us. And so the apostle commands us in Colossians 3:13, "Forgive whatever grievances you may have against one another." Again we see the Bible's realism: even brothers and sisters in Christ will sin against each other. Paul then issues God's vertical standard for all horizontal forgiveness: "Forgive as the Lord forgave you" (v. 13; cf. Eph. 4:32).

We will explore forgiveness in chapters 8 and 9. There we will see that God's forgiveness of us is his decision, declaration, and promise to not hold our sins against us but to graciously hold them against Jesus as our substitute. In fact, God's forgiveness emerges as a major theme here in Colossians. In chapter 1 Paul recalls, "For [God] has rescued us from the dominion of darkness and brought us into the kingdom of the Son he loves, in whom we have redemption, the forgiveness of sins" (Col. 1:13–14). In chapter 2, he rehearses more details, "When you were dead in your sins and in the uncircumcision of your sinful nature, God made you alive with Christ. He forgave us all our sins, having canceled the written code, with its regulations, that was against us and that stood opposed to us; he took it away, nailing it to the cross" (Col. 2:13–14). He forgave us all our sins; therefore we should forgive others their sins.

8. Clothe Yourselves with Love

In Colossians 3:14 Paul concludes his list, "And over all these virtues put on love, which binds them all together in perfect unity." The apostle prioritizes love—our self-sacrificial giving for the other person's best— as the most important virtue, the supreme relational grace. The binding image here apparently pictures love as that outer garment that holds the other seven articles of clothing in place.

Character Qualities or Relational Graces?

When we read lists of Christlike qualities like Colossians 3:12–14, it is vital to understand that these passages are not just inner character qualities or individualistic virtues. They are relational graces, part and parcel of what it means to live in relationship with others. In other words, they are not personal qualities per se but personal qualities displayed toward others. (For example, self-control is not merely inward; it is an inward attitude that relates to others outwardly.)

We see the same dynamic in similar lists. In Ephesians 4:2, Paul calls us to "be completely humble and gentle; be patient, bearing with one another in love." Like those in Colossians 3 above, these are not desert-island, individualistic ideals, but part of the larger, one-body context in Ephesians 4:1–6 of peace and unity. That's why verse 3 continues, "Make every effort to keep the unity of the Spirit through the bond of peace." Humility, gentleness, patience, and forbearance show themselves in relationship to other people and directly nourish church peace.

The famous "fruit of the Spirit" passage shows this dynamic: "But the fruit of the Spirit is love, joy, peace, patience, kindness, goodness, faithfulness, gentleness and self-control" (Gal. 5:22–23). In the context of Galatians 5–6, this ninefold cluster of Spirit-generated graces is not merely inward but also interpersonal. The unit that includes verses 22–23 is flanked by relational emphases both before (5:13–15) and after (5:26—6:2).

116

When the apostle Peter extols sympathy, love, compassion, and humility in 1 Peter 3:8–9, he does so in the context of our relationships: "Finally, all of you, live in harmony with one another; be sympathetic, love as brothers, be compassionate and humble. Do not repay evil with evil or insult with insult, but with blessing, because to this you were called so that you may inherit a blessing." Compassion and humility are one-another graces.

The epistle of James is perhaps best known for its theme of trials, given his opening exhortation: "Consider it pure joy, my brothers, whenever you face trials of many kinds" (James 1:2). A few verses later we read his invitation to seek God's wisdom: "If any of you lacks wisdom, he should ask God, who gives generously to all without finding fault, and it will be given to him" (v. 5). Bible students recognize that James's wisdom reflects the Hebrew concept of wisdom as skillful living before God (more than the Greco-Roman notion of wisdom as chiefly intellectual). What is less obvious is that this skillful handling of trials is not privatized but interpersonal. Notice how James later develops his theme of wisdom.

> Who is wise and understanding among you? Let him show it by his good life, by deeds done in the humility that comes from wisdom. But if you harbor bitter envy and selfish ambition in your hearts, do not boast about it or deny the truth. Such "wisdom" does not come down from heaven but is earthly, unspiritual, of the devil. . . .
>
> But the wisdom that comes from heaven is first of all pure; then peace-loving, considerate, submissive, full of mercy and good fruit, impartial and sincere. Peacemakers who sow in peace raise a harvest of righteousness. (James 3:13–18)

For James, wise handling of trials requires relational skills and bears peace-loving fruit toward others.

Lastly, consider the most famous list of virtues in the Bible, the 1 Corinthians 13 "love chapter." In this celebrated passage, Paul lists a dozen or so marks of love.

> Love is patient, love is kind. It does not envy, it does not boast, it is not proud. It is not rude, it is not self-seeking, it is not easily angered, it keeps no record of wrongs. Love does not delight in evil but rejoices

with the truth. It always protects, always trusts, always hopes, always perseveres. (vv. 4–7)

What is the setting for these qualities? While printed wedding programs popularly feature this text, these verses are not primarily about romance or marital love. Paul wrote to Christians in Corinth who were disputing with and judging one another over church matters.

Moreover, each one of these terms in the original Greek text is a verb. Our English language limits us; we cannot speak of love that "patiences" or "kinds" because we have no such verbs. The best we can do is to make these Greek verbs into English adjectives and supply a linking verb like "is." Yet as writing experts tell us, translating verbs into adjectives often weakens their force. The words become abstractions—a static list of qualities—not concrete ways that love energetically acts in the trenches of conflict. Instead, in Paul's context, these love words carry the flavor of relational skills more than character virtues. Christlike love "patiences and kinds" (action verbs) people that annoy and mistreat us.

Practical Put-on Steps

How should we cultivate these eight attitudes in Colossians 3:12–14 (or the other graces in the other passages above)? The starting place is to select a passage and the specific attitude or quality that you wish to work on. Then pursue one or more of the following practical assignments for each attitude: (I will use compassion, the first in Col. 3:12, as an example.)

1. Reflect on narrative passages in the Bible that picture this quality. Each attitude in verses 12–14 is perfectly and supremely demonstrated in God, especially in the Gospel accounts of Jesus, and genuinely (albeit imperfectly) reflected in his followers. What does God's compassion look like in Exodus 2:23–25 (and 3:7–10), Psalm 103, or Nehemiah 9? How does Jesus show his compassion in the passages listed in footnote 6 above? How does David deal compassionately with Saul and his surviving household throughout 2 Samuel?

2. Pray. Ask God's Spirit to fill you with this (or another) specific attitude. Given the high profile the Lord assigns to these graces, we can confidently believe that he is inclined to hear and answer this prayer.

The same God who promises his Spirit (Luke 11:13) and his wisdom (James 1:5) to those who ask will answer our prayers for specific qualities so that we can pursue peace with others.

3. Identify, confess, and repent of any opposite attitudes you display. In terms of cultivating compassion, where do you see yourself looking down upon, ignoring, or distancing yourself from those who suffer, especially those who suffer the consequences of their own sins? Where do you find yourself judging those who oppose you?

4. Use a Bible concordance or Bible dictionary to do a word study of each quality. (Ask your pastor or another Christian leader for some help in doing this. It can be quite rewarding.)

5. Memorize the list of attitudes in their immediate context (e.g., all of Col. 3:12–14) and call to mind the list when you face conflict. "Father, I belong to you (v. 12a). Help me to respond with compassion, kindness, humility, gentleness, and patience (v. 12b) right now." Posting these verses at your desk, on your bathroom mirror, on the kitchen sink, and on your dashboard will furnish constant reminders.

6. In your conflict situation, envision, list, and carry out concrete action steps that demonstrate the specific attitude. What would compassion look like in this specific relationship? Brainstorm a list. Think of what it would look like in each of your relationships; the specifics often will vary. For example, one woman mentioned her efforts to move the driver's seat back after she uses the car that her taller family members often drive.

7. Enlist prayer, counsel, and accountability from fellow Christians. Admit to them your need for greater compassion. Ask them to pray for you. Invite their practical advice. And as they see evidences of compassion, or the opposite, invite them to notify you.

8. Keep a journal of your successes and failures in cultivating the attitude you are working on. Daily or near-daily entries will raise your consciousness about the specific quality. You will likely find that writing your successes and failures in a prayer journal format ("Dear Lord" more than "Dear Diary" or "Dear Self") will be most helpful.

9. Let God's grace propel you. Continually recall your chosen, holy, loved, forgiven identity. Since each desired quality in its biblical context flows from your calling and identity in Christ, be sure to dwell on what God in Christ has done, is doing, and will do both in you and for you.

Conclusion

Is it possible to change? Can we really clothe ourselves with new attitudes? The good news from Colossians 3 is yes. The chapter is loaded with God's assurances. We are God's new people, capable of growth and change: "you have been raised with Christ" (v. 1) and "your life is now hidden with Christ in God" (v. 3). In your conversion to Jesus and your union with him, "you have taken off your old self with its practices and have put on the new self" (vv. 9–10). You are his chosen, holy, loved, forgiven people (vv. 12–13).

Moreover, God has already begun the work in us. Paul tells us that this new self, with the eight Christlike new-to-us attitudes above, "is being renewed in knowledge in the image of its Creator" (v. 10). The Lord is now actively transforming us into the image of his Son, an image marked by compassion, kindness, humility, gentleness, patience, forbearance, forgiveness, and love.

Perhaps you've heard the old acronym concerning computer data, GIGO: Garbage In, Garbage Out. If you input erroneous data, you will receive erroneous results. However, Colossians 3 signals another kind of GIGO: Grace In, Grace Out. While we are not computers, the ever-powerful, always-efficient grace of God has penetrated our lives through Jesus and his Spirit. This very grace of God that we have received allows us to convey grace to others—compassion, kindness, and so on. The divine grace that changes us produces in us expressions of grace toward others. We can summarize this gospel dynamic in pairs like these: grace in, grace out; grace received, grace radiating; grace inhaled, grace exhaled; and grace acquired, grace dispersed.

Therefore, the Lord calls us to clothe ourselves with the same attitudes he is forming within us. Just as we would not think about going to work or school or church without getting dressed, so we must not start our day or move through our day without donning the clothing of Jesus. This will radically change the way we approach relational conflict.

For Personal Reflection or Group Discussion

1. How do God's choice, possession, and love of you change the way you think about your identity? What does this mean for the relational trials you are facing right now?

2. Select one attitude in the above lists and follow the counsel in the "Practical Put-on Steps" above. How might growing in this area help you in your conflicted relationships?

3. Think of your local church or your small group. Which of the qualities discussed above does your church or group as a whole tend to demonstrate well? How can you affirm others in these areas?

4. On the other hand, which qualities does your group need to develop? How can you demonstrate those qualities in ways that encourage and model their development in your group?

8

To Forgive or Not to Forgive

Forgiving on Two Levels

Everyone says forgiveness is a lovely idea until they have something to forgive.
C. S. Lewis

And when you stand praying, if you hold anything against anyone, forgive him.
Jesus in Mark 11:25

If your brother sins, rebuke him, and if he repents, forgive him.
Jesus in Luke 17:3

Although leaving home to enter college can intimidate a high school graduate, Cindy's fears lessened greatly when she learned that her best friend, Liz, chose the same school. Their decision to room together made the move doubly comfortable. Both were Christians and had prayed about their choice of colleges and about rooming together. Their youth pastor and their parents deemed it an ideal setup.

In the initial months Cindy and Liz faced the common challenges that all roommates must work through, especially in a one-room arrangement: Who would do what cleaning chores and when? When would the lights go off each night and the alarm clocks go on each morning? When would the TV be on, and when would they guard quiet times for study? What food items were fair game to share, and which were hands-off? Cindy and Liz learned to navigate these issues with little conflict, and the fall semester went well.

At the start of the second semester Cindy started dating Justin. Liz sometimes hung out with both of them, but at other times she felt like a third wheel. It was awkward at times, but Liz and Cindy managed.

Cindy's relationship with Justin continued for several months and her affection for him grew, despite some nagging doubts about Justin's level of commitment. Then, in late April, things took a sharp turn. Another friend told Cindy that on the previous evening she saw Justin and Liz together at an off-campus restaurant, on a night that Justin said he planned to study at the library and Liz said she planned to hang out with some other friends.

Cindy immediately confronted Liz, hoping against hope for a plausible explanation. But her hopes were dashed. Liz instantly admitted, with tears, that she and Justin did go out. She told Cindy that she was sorry for lying to her and for going out with him, that it was a mistake, that it was something she deeply regretted, and that she would never do it again. Cindy was silent. She then called Justin and asked him what he had done the night before. He lied. Cindy then confronted him with what her friend had reported and Liz had admitted. Justin was quiet and far from apologetic. His lame "I'm sorry" was followed with a defensive "but I'm not sure we shouldn't feel some freedom to see others."

Cindy was both enraged and heartbroken. In one incident of betrayal she had lost both her boyfriend and her best friend.

"Everyone says forgiveness is a lovely idea," remarked C. S. Lewis, "until they have something to forgive." Lewis described forgiveness—"this terrible duty of forgiving our enemies"—as the most unpopular Christian virtue, yet one that lies at the heart of the Christian's calling.[1] Cindy certainly concurred.

In our previous chapter we focused on eight grace attitudes in Colossians 3:12–14 that are indispensable for loving others and resolving conflict. Near the top in our pursuit of peace is forgiveness. "Bear with each other and forgive whatever grievances you may have against one another. Forgive as the Lord forgave you" (Col. 3:13). So important is the ministry of forgiveness that we will

---

The Path for Pursuing Peace

Step 1. Please God
Step 2. Repent
Step 3. Love the person
  A. Attitudes of grace
  B. Forgive
  C. Confront
  D. Serve

---

[1]C. S. Lewis, *Mere Christianity* (San Francisco: HarperCollins, 2001), 115.

explore it in both this chapter and the next. It is a major theme through-out the Bible.[2]

As we approach the topic of forgiveness, we need to consider the Bible's two major categories: God's forgiveness of us (vertical) and our forgiveness of others (horizontal).[3] Let's begin with God's forgiveness of those who belong to him, and then we will see how this vertical forgiveness empowers our horizontal forgiveness of others.

God's Forgiveness of Us in Christ

What is God's forgiveness? We can define it as God's decision, decla-ration, and promise to those who believe in Jesus Christ to not hold our sins against us because of Jesus Christ. Citing the new covenant vision of Jeremiah 31:34, Hebrews 8:12 summarizes the nature of God's forgiveness as a promise.

> For I will forgive their wickedness
> and will remember their sins no more.

God's forgiveness is a decision he makes, part of his eternal plan of redemption. He chose to send his Son to die on the cross to offer for-giveness for all who would repent and believe in him, and he actually grants that forgiveness—declaring them not guilty in his eyes—when they do repent and believe. Furthermore, God not only decides to forgive; he declares it. He tells us. God doesn't leave us guessing; we don't have to wonder how he looks at us. In the Bible, God's written Word, we read the gospel message and its promises and invitations. And in the oral proclamations by his faithful gospel ministers, we hear those same promises and invitations. We are not left with a symbolic cross or a bare set of historic facts; in the gospel message

---

[2]Gen. 50:15–21; Pss. 25:7; 32; 51; 103:8–12; 130:3–4; Prov. 17:9; 19:11; Isa. 1:18; 38:17; 43:25; 44:22; Jer. 31:31–34; 50:20; Mic. 7:18–20; Matt. 6:12–15; 18:15–17, 21–35; 26:27–29; Mark 11:25; Luke 7:36–50; 17:3–4; 23:34; 24:46–47; Acts 2:36–41; 7:60; Eph. 1:7; 4:31–32; Col. 1:13–14; 2:13–14; 3:13–14; 1 Pet. 4:8.

[3]While some people speak of "forgiving yourself," self-forgiveness is not a biblical concept and can be best understood as a confusion of our first category, God's forgive-ness of us. See Robert D. Jones, *Forgiveness: "I Just Can't Forgive Myself"* (Phillipsburg, NJ: P&R, 2000), for a counseling resource that addresses this problem from a biblical perspective.

we have a divine explanation for the meaning of Jesus's cross, burial, and resurrection.

Yet God's forgiveness goes deeper still. God promises to not hold our sins against us. The parallelism in Hebrews 8:12 is instructive: the Lord's pledge to "forgive their wickedness" is immediately paralleled with his pledge to "remember their sins no more." What does it mean for God to remember no more the sins of his people? It doesn't mean that God suffers a memory lapse or has a "senior moment." The all-knowing, all-seeing Creator does not experience amnesia.

The key to understanding this glorious promise lies in the covenantal meaning of this verb "remember." For God to remember something carries covenantal force. For example, Genesis 6–7 records the flood as God's judgment on the people of Noah's day and God's gracious promise to spare Noah, his family, and representative living creatures. As the ark rose higher, more and more people and animals died, and Genesis 7 ends on a somber note. Everyone and everything was dead, except Noah and his passengers, and they were left floating for five months with no visible hope. What about God's promise?

The turning point in the flood narrative then appears: "But God remembered Noah and all the wild animals and the livestock that were with him in the ark, and he sent a wind over the earth, and the waters receded" (Gen. 8:1). God's covenantal remembrance issued in Noah's salvation, and the redemption story continues. The Lord remembers, then redeems.

We see the same covenantal mercy from God toward his people in Egypt. The first chapter of Exodus recalls the Israelites' suffering under the pharaoh's murderous rule. The mistreatment continues into chapter 2. But Exodus 2 ends with a rich ray of hope: "The Israelites groaned in their slavery and cried out, and their cry for help because of their slavery went up to God. God heard their groaning and he remembered his covenant with Abraham, with Isaac and with Jacob" (Ex. 2:23–24). The passage continues in Exodus 3 with the story of God's appearance to Moses in the burning bush and the start of the exodus miracles. But the turning point is God's covenantal remembrance of his promise to Abraham, Isaac, and Jacob. Therefore, the redemption story continues. The Lord remembers, then redeems.

This backdrop helps us understand the power of God's promise in Jeremiah 31:34 and Hebrews 8:12 to not remember our sins. Divine commitment, not divine amnesia, drives God's forgiveness. In the Jeremiah 31 new covenant promise we read of God's covenantal commitment in verse 20 to remember his people. God's pledge in verse 34 to remember our sins no more demonstrates an entailment of this grace: God remembers us but not our sins, in the sense that he does not hold our sins against us.

Finally, our working definition of God's forgiveness roots it in Jesus Christ. God does not ignore the sins of Christians. He punished our sins. But he does not punish *us* for our sins. He punished our substitute, the Lord Jesus, "the Lamb of God, who takes away the sin of the world" (John 1:29). "He himself bore our sins in his body on the tree" (1 Pet. 2:24). "For Christ died for sins once for all, the righteous for the unrighteous, to bring you to God" (1 Pet. 3:18). For this reason, even the common evangelical expression "God forgives us as we are" is insufficient, since "as we are," apart from Jesus, we are sinful, lost, and unrighteous. Instead, God forgives us *as we are in Christ*. In the new covenant we find forgiveness only in a saving-faith connection with Jesus.

Pictures of God's Forgiveness

Suggesting a definition and supporting it with key doctrinal truths and passages is one profitable way to explore biblical forgiveness. Another way is to focus on the various word pictures in Scripture. The Bible is rich with striking metaphors and moving images that fill out the more doctrinal and analytical insights. They add emotion and passion to our understanding.

Let's consider seven biblical pictures, starting with a pair of psalms. In Psalm 103:11–12 we read of the immensity—the stellar height and global width—of God's forgiveness of his people.

> For as high as the heavens are above the earth,
> so great is his love for those who fear him;
> as far as the east is from the west,
> so far has he removed our transgressions from us.

Here the psalmist couples God's infinite love with his immeasurable forgiveness.

Consider also the relief we find in Psalm 130:3–4.

> If you, O LORD, kept a record of sins,
>   O Lord, who could stand?
> But with you there is forgiveness;
>   therefore you are feared.

Not one of us could stand before the living God if he counted our sins against us. But because he doesn't, and because he has *already* counted our sins against his Son, we can stand before him now and on the final day.

The prophet Isaiah also supplies several thrilling images. After exposing Israel's degenerate condition, Isaiah issues a grace-filled invitation.

> "Come now, let us reason together,"
>   says the LORD.
> "Though your sins are like scarlet,
>   they shall be as white as snow;
> though they are red as crimson,
>   they shall be like wool." (Isa. 1:18)

The reasoning together evokes a courtroom scene; God has brought his Israelite hearers to his bar of justice. But in a unique surprise, he promises hope and restoration: the Lord "can change the unchangeable and delete the indelible."[4] Because of God's mercy, the darkness and redness of our sin gives way to the purity, cleanness, and newness of his redeeming work.

Furthermore, Isaiah records the testimony of King Hezekiah.

> In your love you kept me
>   from the pit of destruction;
> you have put all my sins
>   behind your back. (Isa. 38:17)

---

[4]Derek Kidner, "Isaiah," in D. A. Carson, ed., *New Bible Commentary: 21st Century Edition*, 4th ed. (Downers Grove, IL: InterVarsity, 1994), Isa. 1:10–20.

To put something behind your back is to put it out of sight—in effect, to get rid of it.[5] For God to place my sins behind his back is to forgive me, the way I tossed draft versions of this very book behind my back into a paper recycling bin, never to be seen again.

Two more metaphors emerge from Isaiah. Citing the Lord's words, Isaiah 43:24–25 says,

> But you have burdened me with your sins
>   and wearied me with your offenses.

Yet the next words shine expectant hope.

> I, even I, am he who blots out
>   your transgressions, for my own sake,
>   and remembers your sins no more.

To blot out means to "wipe clean," a work that only God can do: "Sin leaves a mark which only the Lord can wipe away. The verbal form here is a participle, making this ability to wipe sin's stain clean a divine attribute."[6] Isaiah 44:22 paints an additional picture. Citing the Lord again, Isaiah writes,

> I have swept away your offenses like a cloud,
>   your sins like the morning mist.
> Return to me,
>   for I have redeemed you.

Just as dark clouds block heaven from earth, so our sins separate us from God. However, like a mighty wind that clears the stormy sky, the Lord sweeps away our sins. Far from being permanent, our sins remain a passing memory.

---

[5] Two negative uses describe Israel's putting God and his law behind their back: "Therefore this is what the Sovereign Lord says: Since you have forgotten me and thrust me behind your back, you must bear the consequences of your lewdness and prostitution" (Ezek. 23:35); "They put your law behind their backs" (Neh. 9:6).

[6] J. Alec Motyer, *Isaiah: An Introduction and Commentary*, Tyndale Old Testament Commentaries (Downers Grove, IL: InterVarsity, 1999), 309.

In his closing words the prophet Micah brings more color to our panoramic view of our pardoning God. Notice how Micah mixes declarations of pardon and forgiveness with vivid metaphor.

> Who is a God like you,
>> who pardons sin and forgives the transgression
>> of the remnant of his inheritance?
> You do not stay angry forever
>> but delight to show mercy.
> You will again have compassion on us;
>> you will tread our sins underfoot
>> and hurl all our iniquities into the depths of the sea.
> You will be true to Jacob,
>> and show mercy to Abraham,
> as you pledged on oath to our fathers
>> in days long ago. (Mic. 7:18–20)

The passage echoes the many terms found in God's grace-filled self-revelation to Moses in Exodus 34:6–7: "The LORD, the LORD, the compassionate and gracious God, slow to anger, abounding in love and faithfulness, maintaining love to thousands, and forgiving wickedness, rebellion and sin." We find the ultimate fulfillment in Jesus Christ, who has brought us "grace and truth" (John 1:17).[7]

The promise of forgiveness in verse 18 is based in verse 20 on God's covenantal promise, his oath promised to Abraham (cf. Heb. 6:13–20). Between the promised pardon (Mic. 7:18) and the oath (7:20), Micah sandwiches a pair of word pictures. First, God "will tread our sins underfoot"—a picture of military victory, of God conquering and subduing our sins. "Sin is pictured as an enemy that God conquers and liberates us from."[8] God stamps out our sins the way a child stamps out an ant hill. Second, God "hurls all our iniquities into the depths of the sea." His forgiveness is an active work: he "hurls" our sins. It is

---

[7]Leslie C. Allen, *The Books of Joel, Obadiah, Jonah and Micah*, The New International Commentary on the Old Testament (Toronto: Hodder and Stoughton, 1976), 403; Ralph L. Smith and David A. Hubbard, eds., *Micah–Malachi*, Word Biblical Commentary (Waco, TX: Word, 1984), 59; and D. A. Carson, *The Gospel According to John*, The Pillar New Testament Commentary (Grand Rapids: Eerdmans, 1991), 129.

[8]Kenneth L. Barker, *Micah, Nahum, Habakkuk, Zephaniah*, The New American Commentary (Nashville, TN: Broadman & Holman, 2001), 134–35.

comprehensive: "all our iniquities." And it is final, complete, and irreversible: "into the depths of the sea." Again we hear echoes of Exodus—the victory song of Moses.

> Pharaoh's chariots and his army
>> he has hurled into the sea.
> The best of Pharaoh's officers
>> are drowned in the Red Sea.
> The deep waters have covered them;
>> they sank to the depths like a stone. (Ex. 15:4–5)

Things hurled into the depth of the sea—whether corpses dumped by the bad guys in mobster movies or our sins removed by God—cannot be recovered.

One more prophetic image appears in Jeremiah 50:20. The text begins with words that mark a new covenant prediction: "In those days, at that time." It then proceeds with a stunning picture of God's pardoning grace.

> Search will be made for Israel's guilt,
>> but there will be none,
> and for the sins of Judah,
>> but none will be found,
>> for I will forgive the remnant I spare.

As we read this promise in light of the new covenant—Jesus's death and resurrection—the reasons for our forgiveness become clear: search for our sins was indeed once made by God, and our sins were indeed found. But they were not found on us; they were found on the person of Jesus our substitute, who hung on the cross and bore our sins in our place. On that day, God the Father searched for our sins, found them, and put to death our Lord Jesus, "the Lamb of God, who takes away the sin of the world!" (John 1:29).

Transition: God's Forgiveness as Our Model and Motive for Forgiving Others

One major implication flowing from God's forgiveness of us is our duty to forgive others. The Bible tightly connects the two: "Be kind and compassionate to one another, forgiving each other, just as in Christ God forgave you" (Eph. 4:32). "Bear with each other and forgive whatever grievances you may have against one another. Forgive as the Lord forgave you" (Col. 3:13). As we will see in the next chapter, no one has sinned against us as much as we have sinned against God. Yet Jesus teaches us in Matthew 18 that God's forgiveness of our own massive sin debt should compel us to show the same mercy to others. God's forgiveness of us serves as our motive (we forgive *because* he forgave us) and our model (we forgive *in the way* he forgave us) for forgiving others. With the help of God's Spirit and the power of his enabling grace, God's forgiveness of us fuels us and frees us to forgive our offenders. It pushes us to pardon others the way God has pardoned us.

Forgiving Others on Two Levels

As we transition to address God's call for us to forgive others, we begin with a common dilemma that biblical Christians face: Should we forgive unrepentant offenders? Does God command me to forgive that person who sinned against me, even if he is not repentant? Evangelical writers and teachers give varying answers to this question. Some contend that we should forgive offenders unconditionally, even if they do not repent. Others assert that offenders must repent before we forgive them.

With slight tongue-in-cheek, let me suggest a clear, unambiguous, and definite answer to our question: yes and no! Why the dual answer? Because it all depends on how one defines forgiveness. Figure 5 proposes two kinds of forgiveness. We can describe the first level—the bottom level—as attitudinal, heart, or dispositional forgiveness. The second level—the top level—can be called transacted, granted, or relational forgiveness. Level 1 is foundational and prerequisite to Level 2. Level 2 flows from and follows Level 1. We always start with Level 1.

Figure 5. Forgiving others on two levels

| Level 2 |
| Transacted, Granted, Relational Forgiveness |

| Level 1 |
| Attitudinal, Heart, Dispositional Forgiveness |

Table 1. Contrasting the two levels of forgiveness

Level 1 Forgiveness: Attitudinal, Heart, Dispositional	Level 2 Forgiveness: Transacted, Granted, Relational
Jesus's command in Mark 11:25	Jesus's command in Luke 17:3b–4
Jesus's prayer in Luke 23:34a	God's answer in Acts 2:36–41
Vertical focus: between me and God	Horizontal focus: between me and the offender
To release bitterness from my heart: internal	To reconcile my relationship with the offender: relational
Unconditional: independent of the offender's repentance	Conditional: dependent on the offender's repentance
Commitments to God, in God's presence (1) to release the offender from my judgment and entrust him to God, (2) to empty my heart of bitterness, (3) to be ready to grant Level 2 forgiveness and reconcile the relationship, if the offender repents.	Commitments to the repentant offender, in the offender's presence:[1] I will not raise the forgiven offense (1) to myself (dwell, brood), (2) to others (gossip), (3) to you (use against you later).

[1] Ken Sande, *The Peacemaker: A Biblical Guide to Resolving Personal Conflict*, 3rd ed. (Grand Rapids: Baker, 2004), 209–10, offers an expanded version of this, which he calls the four promises of forgiveness: (1) I will not dwell on your offense; (2) I will not talk to others about your offense; (3) I will not bring up your offense and use it against you; and (4) I will not allow your offense to stand between us or hinder our personal relationship.

Table 1 contrasts these two levels along the lines of several contrasting Bible texts above. In Mark 11:25 Jesus says, "And when you stand praying, if you hold anything against anyone, forgive him, so that your Father in heaven may forgive you your sins." The scene pictures private prayer—the believer alone before God, conversing with his heavenly Father. The other person is not present; no repentance or relational contact is presumed. We are simply alone before God dealing with our heart attitudes toward the sinner and internally releasing him—unconditionally—from his debt to us. (As we will see below, elsewhere Jesus calls us to go to this person, but not in this context.)

On the other hand, Jesus presents a Level 2 picture in Luke 17:3–4: "If your brother sins, rebuke him, and if he repents, forgive him. If he sins against you seven times in a day, and seven times comes back to you and says, 'I repent,' forgive him." Does the conditional element surprise you? In our age of religious tolerance, we might have expected Jesus to say, "If your brother sins, forgive him." But Jesus surprises us. He does not want us to settle for a form of forgiveness that does not address the actual offense. Instead, he gives priority to a restored relationship—a reconciliation marked by the offender's repentance and the offended party's transacted forgiveness.

Or consider our Lord's words on the cross, probably the first of Jesus's seven sayings: "Father, forgive them, for they do not know what they are doing" (Luke 23:34a). How did Jesus view those who put him to death? He evidences an unconditional Level 1 heart attitude of forgiveness toward the perpetrators by asking his Father to forgive them. Does this mean that Jesus declared them to be forgiven? No, this was a prayer to his Father, an intercessory prayer demonstrating Jesus's heart of mercy. As J. C. Ryle observes, "His own racking agony of body did not make Him forget others: the first of His seven sayings on the cross was a prayer for the souls of His murderers."[9] We find the church's first martyr, Stephen, following his Lord's example: "While they were stoning him, Stephen prayed, 'Lord Jesus, receive my spirit.' Then he fell on his knees and cried out, 'Lord, do not hold this sin against them.' When he had said this, he fell asleep" (Acts 7:59–60).

Was Jesus's prayer answered? While we see in the crucifixion accounts in the four Gospels several who did repent and believe (e.g., the centurion in Luke 23:47), most apparently did not. But several writers have suggested that in Luke's next inspired book, Acts, he shows a further, dramatic answer to Jesus's prayer, at least among the Jews who asked for him to be crucified. Fifty days later, in Acts 2:38, the apostle Peter offers God's conditional forgiveness to his Jewish audience: "Repent and be baptized, every one of you, in the name of Jesus Christ for the forgiveness of your sins." Like his instruction in Mark 11:25, Jesus's prayer in Luke 23:34 demonstrates Level 1 attitudinal forgiveness toward his adversaries. Meanwhile, Peter's Acts 2 rebuke of those who killed Jesus, followed by their repentance and God's forgiveness, follows the Level 2 pattern in Luke 17:3–4. (For those interested in thinking further about this two-level distinction, especially for counselors, I have summarized in appendix A the way several other biblical counselors use this same dual approach, albeit with different terminology.)

---

[9]J. C. Ryle, *Expository Thoughts on the Gospels: St. Luke*, vol. 2 (London: James Clarke, 1969), 463.

Carrying Out Attitudinal (Level 1) Forgiveness

Having seen what it means for God to forgive us and the two levels on which we forgive others, how do we carry out these two levels? In this section we will summarize the components of attitudinal forgiveness. In chapter 9 we will unpack six specific gospel-soaked truths that will help us cultivate attitudinal forgiveness, especially when we are tempted to become bitter. In chapter 10 we will then focus on carrying out transacted forgiveness, including a discussion of when to overlook (Prov. 19:11) or cover over (1 Pet. 4:8) others' sins (forgiving attitudinally) and when to rebuke or confront (with the goal of granting transactional forgiveness if the person repents).

In all cases, whether the offender repents or not, we must begin with attitudinal forgiveness, always factoring in this unconditional component when responding to anyone who sins against us. It is the proper disposition—the Christian attitude—of all who have been gloriously forgiven by God. What then does it mean to forgive someone in our hearts? Consider three components.

1. Attitudinal forgiveness involves releasing the offender from our judgment, and entrusting him, ourselves, and the situation into God's hands. In forgiveness we decide to stop playing the role of judge. Several passages picture this:

- "But Joseph said to them, 'Don't be afraid. Am I in the place of God?'" (Gen. 50:19).
- "Do not take revenge, my friends, but leave room for God's wrath, for it is written: 'It is mine to avenge; I will repay,' says the Lord" (Rom. 12:19).
- "There is only one Lawgiver and Judge, the one who is able to save and destroy. But you—who are you to judge your neighbor?" (James 4:12).

In other words, we let God be God. By faith we consciously lift the offender and place him before God the righteous Judge. Moreover, like Jesus, when facing mistreatment we entrust ourselves to God our Father:

- "'[Jesus] committed no sin, / and no deceit was found in his mouth.' / When they hurled their insults at him, he did not retaliate; when he suffered, he made no threats. Instead, he entrusted himself to him who judges justly" (1 Pet. 2:22–23).

- "So then, those who suffer according to God's will should commit themselves to their faithful Creator and continue to do good" (1 Pet. 4:19).

2. Attitudinal forgiveness involves emptying our hearts of bitterness. Along with entrusting ourselves and the offender into God's hands, we are called to take responsibility for our own responses. We cannot blame the other party for our sinful anger. The apostle's command is clear and comprehensive: "Get rid of all bitterness, rage and anger, brawling and slander, along with every form of malice" (Eph. 4:31). Paul uses no fewer than six synonyms for bitterness, and he tells us to get rid of them all. We cannot excuse our wrong reactions to being sinned against. Instead, he calls us to forgive: "Be kind and compassionate to one another, forgiving each other, just as in Christ God forgave you" (v. 32). This is the attitude reflected in the famous words of the African American author, educator, and activist Booker T. Washington: "I would permit no man, no matter what his colour might be, to narrow and degrade my soul by making me hate him."[10] While Washington was addressing the evils of racism, his conviction applies powerfully to all forms of mistreatment. Attitudinal forgiveness liberates us from the soul-shrinking notion that blames others for our bitterness.

3. Attitudinal forgiveness involves being ready, in cases of major offenses, to grant Level 2 transacted forgiveness and to reconcile the relationship if the offender repents and seeks reconciliation. In attitudinal forgiveness we long for the relationship to be restored, knowing that only the offender's current impenitence prevents that reconciliation. Attitudinal forgiveness leads us to pray for God to show mercy to the other party, the way Jesus (Luke 23:34) and Stephen (Acts 7:60) prayed for their persecutors. In addition, depending on the severity of the sin, attitudinal forgiveness leads us to take loving steps to rebuke the other person so that transacted forgiveness can be granted and enjoyed by both parties.

Conclusion

Do you remember Cindy in our story above, the college freshman betrayed by both her best friend, Liz, and her boyfriend, Josh? Heart

---

[10]Booker T. Washington, "Making Their Beds before They Could Lie on Them," in *Up from Slavery: An Autobiography* (1901), chap. 11.

forgiveness presented a massive spiritual challenge for her. Cindy's emotions were raw; she cried daily for weeks. But the Lord enabled her to actively place both Josh and Liz into his hands in daily prayer. Along with several of the word pictures above, two biblical truths especially gripped her mind: she remembered how Jesus bore her sins in his body on the tree (1 Pet. 2:24) and how she needed to forgive others as the Lord forgave her (Col. 3:13). Sadly, her efforts to talk with Josh never succeeded. He avoided her for the rest of the semester and transferred to another school for the following fall. With God's help, Cindy was able to apply the gospel truths in this chapter and the next when bad memories about Josh arose. Moreover, she was able to transact forgiveness with Liz.

Forgiving others often presents a huge hurdle for us to clear. The costs are high. How is it possible for us to forgive? Let me close with two overarching answers. First, meditating on the gospel message of God's forgiveness of us moves us to extend this grace toward others. (We will explore this further in the next chapter.) Second, as we seek God in prayer, his Holy Spirit gives us the desire and inner strength to forgive our offenders in the way we have outlined above (Phil. 2:12–13; 4:13; Heb. 4:16; 13:20–21). As we saw in chapter 2, his Spirit alone can enable us—and does enable us—to please God in this specific task of forgiving others.

FOR PERSONAL REFLECTION OR GROUP DISCUSSION

1. Briefly summarize a situation in which you were sinned against. How did the distinction between two levels of forgiveness help you, or how would it have helped you (if you knew and applied it), to treat the offender in godly ways?

2. Imagine that someone has sinned seriously against your good friend but remains unrepentant. How might you advise your friend to cultivate attitudinal forgiveness?

3. Which of the word pictures under "Pictures of God's Forgiveness" above was most encouraging, helpful, or challenging to you? Why?

9

Battling Bitterness by Grace

It's mercy, compassion, and forgiveness I lack, not rationality.
Beatrix Kiddo (Uma Thurman) in Quentin Tarantino's film, *Kill Bill, volume 1*

The servant's master took pity on him, canceled the debt and let him go.
Jesus in Matthew 18:27

Throughout four years of marriage, Carla's relationship with Max's parents had always been distant.[1] But when her mother-in-law, Gail, came for an extended visit, the tension escalated. Gail's comments about Carla's parenting techniques did not sit well. The first correction irritated Carla; the second ignited her. The ensuing days witnessed several verbal clashes. At the end of the visit their parting words were civil, but strained. The breakdown, however, worsened in the following months. Every weekly phone call from Gail to her son only intensified Carla's bitterness. And the problem did not end there. Carla's complaints about Gail migrated into attacks against Max. "Why didn't you stand up to her when she criticized the way I handled our children? How can you speak so sweetly to her on the phone?" Carla's bitterness was increasing and her marriage was deteriorating.

Doug's new job had started well. While serving as a waiter was not his ideal career, the restaurant was well respected and popular, the more elegant menu prices meant good tips, and the owner appreciated Doug's dependability. But after about six months, for reasons unknown to Doug, the boss's mood shifted. Doug's hours were cut, his request to work weekends was ignored, and several newly hired servers were

---

[1] The substance of this chapter first appeared as a booklet by Robert D. Jones, *Freedom from Resentment: Stopping Hurts from Turning Bitter* (Greensboro, NC: New Growth, 2010).

given more favorable shifts. When Doug questioned his boss, the man seemed unapologetic, unsympathetic, and unmoved. Nothing changed. Doug's irritation rose, and sleepless nights followed. He found himself increasingly resentful of his boss and jealous of his coworkers. Bitterness was just around the bend for Doug.

Debbie's first marriage ended disastrously after her husband's repeated infidelity. So her friends and relatives rejoiced when she met Aaron, a caring man marked by constancy and sensitivity. But her dream honeymoon year became a nightmare when Aaron committed adultery. Thankfully, he immediately repented, renewed his marital vows, and proved himself in the ensuing three years to be a solid husband. Sadly, however, Debbie was unable to get over her husband's betrayal, despite his sincere repentance. While she maintained an outer semblance of marital commitment, deep down her heart remained hard.

Do you find yourself relating to Carla, Doug, or Debbie?

There is nothing uglier than bitterness—that inner anger lodged deep in the heart, sometimes known only to the bitter person (and his all-seeing God). Bitterness is *settled* anger, the kind that not merely reacts to someone's offense, but forms a more general and global animosity against the offender himself. Anger responds to an incident: "I'm angry about *what you did*." Bitterness goes deeper to form an attitude—a settled stance or posture—against the perpetrator: "I'm bitter at *you*, because *you are* an evil person." The incident becomes almost secondary.

With most hurts we encounter in our imperfect world, especially small ones, we learn to overlook the offense and forgive the offender. But occasionally we experience a major hurt—an offense that cuts deeply or turns our world upside down—that lingers in our minds and tempts us to become bitter. We might store that hurt in our heart, nurture it, and let it grow to the point where we look with hostility at the offender.

What hope do Carla, Doug, Debbie, you, and I have to escape the sorrow, slavery, and soul impoverishment that resentment brings?

The Path for Pursuing Peace

Step 1. Please God
Step 2. Repent
Step 3. Love the person
  A. Attitudes of grace
  B. Forgive (continued)
  C. Confront
  D. Serve

The answer is found in Jesus. Jesus understands. He is with us. He comes to us in our mistreatment and remains with us to help. He understands mistreatment as one who was sinned against severely. He has been there. The Scriptures tell us that he came to save his own people, but they did not receive him (John 1:11).

> He was despised and rejected by men,
>   a man of sorrows, and familiar with suffering. (Isa. 53:3)

Jesus was sinned against severely: mocked, taunted, punched, spit upon, abandoned, and crucified. This is the Jesus—the mistreated one—who is with us and who is able to help us handle our resentment and overcome our bitterness.

How? The answer is the gospel message of Jesus Christ. In Ephesians 4:31, the apostle Paul calls us to "get rid of all bitterness, rage and anger, brawling and slander, along with every form of malice." The antidote to bitterness? "Be kind and compassionate to one another, forgiving each other, just as in Christ God forgave you" (Eph. 4:32). This verse is the apostle's strategy to battle the bitterness he warns against in the previous verse. He calls us to have our minds consciously controlled by God's forgiveness through Jesus's death on the cross. Grasping the mighty work of our incarnate, crucified, and risen Lord moves us to forgive others.

Let's rehearse six gospel truths that can prevent resentment from building and stop hurts from becoming bitter. With each, we'll also consider the flipside—six realities that mark us when we let resentment arise and fester.

1. The Enormity of God's Love Displayed in the Cross

If we become bitter, we will have forgotten the massive size of the sin debt that God forgave us. Matthew 18:21–35 gives us the greatest story about forgiveness Jesus ever told. The passage begins with Peter's timely question. "Peter came to Jesus and asked, 'Lord, how many times shall I forgive my brother when he sins against me? Up to seven times?'" (v. 21). Peter's suggestion appears generous in light of traditional teaching that recommended three times.

Yet Jesus is not impressed: "I tell you, not seven times, but seventy-seven times" (v. 22). The number seventy-seven (or "seventy times seven"; English translations vary) suggests an unlimited amount, with seven being the number of perfection. Don't count offenses; forgive without limits.

Jesus then illustrates his statement with a story about a king and two of his servants.

> The kingdom of heaven is like a king who wanted to settle accounts with his servants. As he began the settlement, a man who owed him ten thousand talents was brought to him. Since he was not able to pay, the master ordered that he and his wife and his children and all that he had be sold to repay the debt. (vv. 23–25)

Currency-conversion estimates for ten thousand "talents" (coins) range from twelve million to a billion dollars today—in other words, an unpayable sum. Jesus uses a deliberate exaggeration to make his point. The first servant bore an impossible debt. And so he pleaded for mercy. "The servant fell on his knees before him. 'Be patient with me,' he begged, 'and I will pay back everything'" (v. 26).

How did the king respond? "The servant's master took pity on him, canceled the debt and let him go" (v. 27). No conditions, no limitations, no hesitations—the unpayable debt gone with one royal declaration from a merciful king!

But then the parable takes a tragic turn. "When that servant went out, he found one of his fellow servants who owed him a hundred denarii. He grabbed him and began to choke him. 'Pay back what you owe me!' he demanded" (v. 28).

How much was this debt? Scholars tell us that one denarius was the daily wage for a common day laborer. One hundred denarii would equal one hundred days of pay, or approximately one-third of an annual salary. If we think of $18,000 as a low annual wage, then a hundred days would mean $6,000. This, of course, is a significant amount. If I borrowed five dollars from you for lunch on a day when I've forgotten my wallet, you might overlook the question of repayment; if I borrowed $6,000, you'd likely track me down and remind me. That would be a considerable amount, but far less than a multimillion-dollar obligation.

Like us, Jesus's original hearers would have been shocked at the first servant's action. But maybe all is not lost in our story. Maybe, if the second servant implores him, the first servant will soften his heart and reverse his decision.

So with the same words the first servant successfully used to entreat the master, the second servant pleaded, "Be patient with me, and I will pay you back" (v. 29). But the first servant appeared unchanged by the king's mercy to him: "He refused. Instead, he went off and had the man thrown into prison until he could pay the debt" (v. 30). "He refused"—the words chill us! The recipient of incalculable mercy hardened his heart, ignoring the massive size of his own forgiven debt.

Does that trouble you? It should. But you are not alone.

> When the other servants saw what had happened, they were greatly distressed and went and told their master everything that had happened. Then the master called the servant in. "You wicked servant," he said, "I canceled all that debt of yours because you begged me to. Shouldn't you have had mercy on your fellow servant just as I had on you?" In anger his master turned him over to the jailers to be tortured, until he should pay back all he owed. (vv. 31–34)

Jesus then makes his unmistakable point, the point of the parable: we who have been forgiven a mega-debt should forgive others from our hearts. "This is how my heavenly Father will treat each of you unless you forgive your brother from your heart" (v. 35). Failing to forgive invites severe consequences.

People mistreat us, sometimes in horrific ways. What Carla, Doug, and Debbie face is far too common. Spouses cheat. Children rebel. Bosses fire. Friends lie. Pastors fail. Parents abuse. Hurts are real. But how do all these $6,000 offenses against us compare to the multimillion-dollar debt we owed God, which he mercifully canceled? Since birth, and for all our lives, we have failed to love the Lord our God with all our heart, soul, mind, and strength, and our neighbor as ourselves (Matt. 22:37–39). But with one fell swoop—by the death and resurrection of Jesus—God wiped our records clean. Through the cross of Jesus and our faith in him, God removed our transgressions from us "as far as the east is from the west" (Ps. 103:12); he hurled "all our iniquities into the depths of the sea" (Mic. 7:19); he has made our "scarlet" sins "as white as snow" (Isa. 1:18).

Could it be that one reason you find it so hard to forgive is that you have never received God's forgiveness by repenting of your sins and believing in Jesus as your Savior? Or maybe you have yet to grasp the majesty—the enormity—of God's forgiveness of all your many sins. Maybe we simply forget the piercing truth emerging from our Lord's story: no one has ever sinned against you as much as you have sinned against God. If you dwell on your offender's $6,000 debt against you, you will be trapped in bitterness until you die. But if you dwell on God's forgiveness of your multimillion-dollar debt, you will find release and liberty. Being kind, compassionate, and forgiving will remain burdensome for anyone who minimizes the thrilling force of the full pardon Jesus gives.

2. Our Desperate Need for God's Forgiveness

If we become bitter and unforgiving, we will be declaring that we do not need God's forgiveness in our lives. Here's another good reason to forgive others: so God will forgive us! Jesus said, "When you stand praying, if you hold anything against anyone, forgive him, so that your Father in heaven may forgive you your sins" (Mark 11:25). And he instructed his disciples to pray this way, "Forgive us our debts, as we also have forgiven our debtors. . . . For if you forgive men when they sin against you, your heavenly Father will also forgive you. But if you do not forgive men their sins, your Father will not forgive your sins" (Matt. 6:12, 14–15).

Jesus unmistakably states that God's forgiveness of us depends somehow on our forgiving others. We will make no progress in battling bitterness until we take to heart our Lord's clear words: God withholds our forgiveness until we forgive.

In what way? Evangelical Bible scholars handle these conditional texts in two different ways. The first approach contends that when we accept Christ as our Savior, God the Judge declares us righteous, irreversibly forgiving all our sins—past, present, and future—so that none of them will ever condemn us. What happens if we don't forgive others? While he won't disown us (because of Christ) God as our Father *will* frown upon us. Our resentments hinder our relationship with our Father, and only by forgiving others can we clear those clouds. The second approach teaches that forgiving others evidences that we really are Christians. When God saves us, he gives us a new disposition to love him and to love others. But if we are bitter, we invite the fair question of whether we have ever been forgiven of our sins.

Which view is correct? While studying the passage is vital, too often scholars and laypeople alike can get lost in these debates and miss Jesus's point: We must forgive others!

The point becomes clearer when we consider the distressing options: would you rather have a clouded, distant relationship with your heavenly Father or have your salvation legitimately doubted by others? Neither gets my vote. Or would you rather live in the joyful freedom of unhindered communion with God and the confident assurance that you belong to him?

The remedy in either case is the same: forgive others! This one certain constant should constrain us: Jesus wants us to forgive in our hearts all those who have wronged us.

These first two gospel truths struck Doug. As his pastoral counselor shared Matthew 18:21–35, discussed above, Doug realized that his boss's sins against him were far less than Doug's twenty-plus years of sin against God. And then, when Doug read verse 35—"This is how my heavenly Father will treat each of you unless you forgive your brother from your heart"—he saw the danger of clinging to his bitterness. Doug began to grasp the greatness of God's grace and the need to convey that grace to his unfair boss, and the bitterness began to dissipate.

3. Our Ultimate Need for God's Mercy

Our God is a God of matchless mercy, one who delights in showing grace even to those who offend him deeply. His forgiving mercies extend from east to west (Ps. 103:12). He mercifully saves us despite our unrighteous deeds. His mercies are new every morning (Lam. 3:23).

But if we become bitter, we will be declaring that we do not need God's mercy. This third reason parallels the second. We need forgiveness, and we also need mercy.

How might you answer this simple question: On the day of final judgment, do you want to face God with mercy, or without mercy? The point is obvious: we all want almighty God to treat us mercifully. We don't want to stand before him on our own merits. The apostle James tells us how to achieve that final scenario: "Judgment without mercy will be shown to anyone who has not been merciful. Mercy triumphs over judgment!" (James 2:13).

Mercy, of course, always marks the godly person.

> He has showed you, O man, what is good.
>   And what does the LORD require of you?
> To act justly and to love mercy
>   and to walk humbly with your God. (Mic. 6:8)

The godly person loves mercy. He is a merciful person, like God his Father: "Be merciful, just as your Father is merciful" (Luke 6:36).

Shakespeare's heroine Portia understands this in *The Merchant of Venice* as she entreats the evil Shylock to spare the life of his enemy Antonio.

> The quality of mercy is not strain'd,
> It droppeth as the gentle rain from heaven
> Upon the place beneath: it is twice blest;
> It blessed him that gives and him that takes. . . .
> It is an attribute to God himself. (act 4, scene 1)

Mercy toward our enemies is Godlike, coming down from heaven, bringing blessing both to those we forgive and to us who extend it. As our Lord Jesus said, "Blessed are the merciful, for they will be shown mercy" (Matt. 5:7).

4. God's Role and Ours

If we become bitter, we will be assuming God's role as Judge and Avenger. What role do we play when we remain bitter against someone? We are functioning as a judge. We assess the evidence against someone, render a verdict, and declare him guilty. No wonder the apostle James challenges our judgmentalism: "There is only one Lawgiver and Judge, the one who is able to save and destroy. But you—who are you to judge your neighbor?" (James 4:12). Bitter people grab the throne of the one Lawgiver and Judge.

Consider also Paul's well-known words in Romans 12:19: "Do not take revenge, my friends, but leave room for God's wrath, for it is written: 'It is mine to avenge; I will repay,' says the Lord." Most people know revenge is wrong; fewer people understand why. The reason is not because evil acts do not warrant justice. They do. The point of the passage is that this is God's job, not ours: "It is mine to avenge; I will repay."

In fact, there are two commands in this passage, not just one. We all know the negative command: "Do not take revenge." Yet the positive command is equally vital: "Leave room for God's wrath." We must trust God to be God, to let God be angry for us. Don't avenge; trust the righteous Avenger to bring justice in his time and in his way.

The Old Testament story of Joseph displays these truths memorably. In Genesis 50, Joseph's brothers feared that their now highly powerful brother might avenge their treacherous acts committed against him in their younger years. As long as their father Jacob lived, Joseph would not harm them. The chapter, however, opens with Jacob's funeral. They attempted to appease Joseph by seeking his forgiveness, but the timing seems suspiciously contrived, and they apparently fabricated their deceased father's words. When they arrived, they threw themselves down before Joseph as slaves.

Joseph's merciful response reflected his knowledge of God and God's sovereign ways: "Don't be afraid. Am I in the place of God?" (Gen. 50:19). Joseph understood the truth of Romans 12 and James 4, that judgment is God's role, not ours. As the ensuing verses show, Joseph could extend grace because his God was in control of his life.

What should you do if resentment builds? Release your offender from your judgment and entrust him to God. To paraphrase the counsel of the late Presbyterian pastor D. James Kennedy, "Descend the staircase in your heart, open the prison door, unlock the chains, and let him out of the dungeon of your soul."

This truth particularly pierced Carla. Amid her anger against her mother-in-law, Carla became distressed over what she was becoming and the way she allowed Gail's phone calls to produce in her such an adversarial stance toward both Gail and Max. The passage that God's Spirit used to expose Carla's sin was Romans 14:9–10: "For this very reason, Christ died and returned to life so that he might be the Lord of both the dead and the living. You, then, why do you judge your brother? Or why do you look down on your brother? For we will all stand before God's judgment seat."

There it was, staring her in the face. Jesus Christ alone died and rose to become the Lord and Judge over both Carla and Gail. That meant for Carla that she had no right to usurp Jesus's role as Judge over Gail. She was not Gail's Lord. Carla had also failed to recognize that Gail's sins were precisely the sins for which Jesus died—the same blood spilt to cover Carla's sins also covered her mother-in-law's sin. Carla must not judge someone for whom Jesus died. Moreover, she realized that one day she would stand before the Lord for her own sin, including her condemnatory attitude toward her mother-in-law. Convicted of her sin, Carla repented and found the freedom of God's forgiveness.

5. The Dual Nature of the Offender's Sin

If we become bitter, we will forget that as a sinner the offender is deceived and enslaved by his sin. How do you look at the person who offended you? Scripture presents a profound tension in describing sinners. On the one hand, we are rebellious and disobedient.

> There is no one righteous, not even one;
>> there is no one who understands,
>> no one who seeks God.
> All have turned away,
>> they have together become worthless;
> there is no one who does good,
>> not even one. (Rom. 3:10–12)

"Everyone who sins breaks the law; in fact, sin is lawlessness" (1 John 3:4). We usually have little problem viewing our offenders this way.

But the Bible brings a balancing perspective. People who sin against us are not only rebels and lawbreakers; they are also deceived and enslaved. Jesus speaks plainly to the Pharisees: "Everyone who sins is a slave to sin" (John 8:34). The apostle Peter called false teachers "slaves of depravity," observing that "a man is a slave to whatever has mastered him" (2 Pet. 2:19). Proverbs 5:22 declares,

> The evil deeds of a wicked man ensnare him;
> the cords of his sin hold him fast.

Sin enslaves. It deceives. It blinds.

Nowhere does this truth appear more strikingly than at the cross. Our Lord Jesus pleads for his perpetrators, "Father, forgive them, for they do not know what they are doing" (Luke 23:34). Amazing! Jesus views his crucifiers as self-deceived and ignorant, and he mercifully prays for their forgiveness. Similarly, Paul explains how unbelievers are blind to God's secret wisdom, the gospel: "None of the rulers of this age understood it, for if they had, they would not have crucified the Lord of glory" (1 Cor. 2:8). If their blind eyes had seen Jesus's glory, they would not have killed him.

How does this transform the way we look at offenders? Let me say this delicately, especially if someone has sinned against you severely. A Christlike perspective on your offender includes recognizing that person's slavery and self-deception. It means not taking that person's sin against you too personally.

As a pastor and counselor, I have been privileged to help couples restore their marriages after adultery. That has meant interviewing men and women who have been unfaithful to their partner. I have never heard a husband say, "Well, Bob, here's what happened. I woke up one morning and decided on a whim that I wanted to destroy my wife's life. So I thought about it. How should I do it? Hmm, I know. I'll have an affair. Yeah, that's the ticket. Hmm, but with whom? Let me think. I know. I'll go sleep with . . ."

That's not the way it typically happens. Instead, the man pursues his own desires—which he and our culture wrongly call needs—desires for control, for power, for affection, for admiration, or for something new or daring or illicit. Maybe another woman shows him attention. She laughs at his jokes and thinks, *He's so nice.* Gradually—and blindly—he continues down this path until it turns sexual. But ultimately it was not about his wife's supposed failures, or even about his preference for the other woman. It was about him and his pride, self-centeredness, and demands. His sin enslaved him and blinded him to his God and to his wife.

Please understand. Such a man remains entirely responsible for his decisions. He is rebellious and disobedient—to be judged (by God, not us). But he is also deceived and enslaved—to be pitied. In fact, one of the spectacular, Godlike turning points for the wife occurs right here: along with her (understandable) struggle with anger, she begins to feel a surprising measure of Christlike compassion for this man who betrayed her. She sees how he has blindly followed his own way. She learns not to take his sin too personally, and to see his sin as chiefly not against her but against God. And while she has never committed adultery, she understands that both his adultery and her own multimillion-dollar sins arise from the same selfish root.

> We all, like sheep, have gone astray,
>   each of us has turned to his own way;
> and the LORD has laid on him [Christ]
>   the iniquity of us all. (Isa. 53:6)

This was the masterstroke for Debbie. She came to see that her three years of bitterness resulted from her three years of blindness. She failed to see Aaron as God saw him. As Debbie's Christian friend helped her to see Aaron properly, and as she encouraged Debbie to talk to her husband, Debbie was able to hear for the first time—with compassion—Aaron's self-deceived struggle with his own sin. She later testified: "I struggled for several years in bondage to my anger. I wrongly believed that to forgive Aaron meant to condone his affair and agree with his justifying rationale. But God began to show me from his Word that Aaron's sin was deeper than what he did to me. Aaron was blind and self-deceived, an out-of-control, shepherdless man who desperately needed Jesus. My anger turned to pity as I prayed for him and asked God to rescue him from himself."

6. Our Own Fallibility

If we become bitter, we will be forgetting that as sinners we too are capable of the same sins, and that the same root sins may already reside in us. Through the passages considered, Carla began to see another distressing pattern that the cross alone could shatter. As she contemplated her mother-in-law's criticisms of her, Carla had to admit she was doing the same thing. While Gail criticized Carla, Carla responded by criticizing Gail and also by criticizing Max.

Through her pastor's biblical counseling, Carla came to realize that when sinned against by others, we can easily forget that we too are sinners, and apart from sheer grace we are no better than our offenders. In our resentment against others we forget that our own hearts are "deceitful above all things and beyond cure" (Jer. 17:9). Aware of the power of remaining sin, the writer to the Hebrews reminds the church, "See to it, brothers, that none of you has a sinful, unbelieving heart that turns away from the living God. But encourage one another daily, as long as it is called Today, so that none of you may be hardened by sin's deceitfulness" (Heb. 3:12–13). This text hit Carla right between the eyes. Her bitterness against Max's mom was actually a step toward spiritual self-destruction. Unchecked, it would destroy her. Even professing Christians are not immune to the dangers of a deceitful heart that overlooks its own sin and judges others.

What does this danger look like? It begins with sentiments like these: "I would never do to someone else what he did to me!" "I can't believe he did that; I would never do that to him!" When we say things like that, surely the Lord winces. Are we really so sure that we couldn't do the same thing? How confident should we be that we would never commit any specific sin? Given the same background and life models, how can we know with such certainty that we would never do the same thing that the offender did to us? How do we really know that, given the same circumstances and environment, and the same temptations and provocations, we would not commit the same hurtful act?

Proverbs 16:18 alerts us to our grave danger.

> Pride goes before destruction,
> a haughty spirit before a fall.

The apostle Paul likewise warns, "If you think you are standing firm, be careful that you don't fall!" (1 Cor. 10:12). In our bitterness we naively pretend moral superiority and invulnerability.

Few have captured this concept more famously than the English Reformation pastor and martyr, John Bradford (1510–1555). From his prison cell in the tower of London he saw a criminal being led to execution for his crimes. Bradford's words are memorable: "There but for the grace of God, goes John Bradford." Using the gospel to battle bitterness means that, apart from God's grace, we are no better than the man or woman who has sinned against us.

Conclusion

Only Jesus Christ can deeply address your hurts, sever the roots of resentment, and melt any bitterness forming in your soul. Let me suggest a specific step to help you in your battle against bitterness: Review the six truths above, one at a time, prayerfully. Reread the first truth and look up the Bible passages referenced. Reflect on their message, and pick a verse to memorize and meditate on. Then write a prayer to the Lord based on that truth—a prayer that honestly confesses your resentment before him and thoughtfully seeks to apply the Bible to your battle. On the next day, repeat the same procedure for the next gospel truth. Continue to do the same each day, one truth per day. After your six days, repeat the same six-day cycle again, reviewing the same passages and memory verses, but writing new prayers.

Will this activity help? Can your battle against bitterness really succeed? Yes, in time. Carla, Doug, and Debbie found victory. God's grace in Jesus can heal your soul by drawing you closer to him. It is my prayer that our Lord will use these gospel truths to help you progressively chip away at your settled anger—that with the Holy Spirit's help you might "get rid of all bitterness" and "be kind and compassionate to one another, forgiving each other, just as in Christ God forgave you" (Eph. 4:31–32). As you marinate your mind in the gospel message, you can expect God to begin changing your view of those who have sinned against you.

For Personal Reflection or Group Discussion

1. Complete the practical assignment included in the conclusion above.

2. Which one of the above six truths is most helpful for you in being able to guard against or overcome resentment? Which one seems most difficult to apply?

3. Write a prayer to the Lord in which you weave in one or more of the six truths above, and seek his help to guard against or overcome resentment.

10

Redeeming the Art of Rebuke and Granting Forgiveness

When and How to Confront and Forgive

> Better is open rebuke
> than hidden love.
> Wounds from a friend can be trusted,
> but an enemy multiplies kisses.
> Proverbs 27:5–6

> A man's wisdom gives him patience;
> it is to his glory to overlook an offense.
> Proverbs 19:11

There are ministry words in the Bible that everyone loves, words like *serve, greet,* and *encourage.* There are other words that convey things hard to do, but we favor them nonetheless—words like *forgive, exhort,* and *prefer one another.* But there is one ministry word that few people warm up to. We don't enjoy doing it, and we don't enjoy receiving it. It's *rebuke.* Stop and think about the last time, if ever, someone asked you to lunch to rebuke you. I can probably predict your level of excitement.

Contrast our aversion to rebuke with the way God's Word commends it. Jesus equates it with love: "Those whom I love I rebuke and discipline" (Rev. 3:19). Our Lord expresses true love for his people through caring confrontation. We have a lot to learn as his disciples. While words like *rebuke, reprove, confront,* and *admonish* are unpopular in our society and even (sadly) among most Christians, God commands us to minister to each other in these ways to reflect our true love for each other.

The Path for Pursuing Peace

Step 1. Please God
Step 2. Repent
Step 3. Love the person
  A. Attitudes of grace
  B. Forgive
  C. Confront
  D. Serve

Where does rebuke fit into our biblical peacemaking process? Based on God's grace, we commit to please the God who has saved us (Step 1, chap. 3). We examine our heart sins and behavioral sins before the Lord, and then we confess them to the Lord, and we confess our behavioral sins to the other person (Step 2, chaps. 4–6). We then seek to love the other person by displaying Christlike grace and attitudinal forgiveness, guarding ourselves against bitterness (Step 3, chaps. 7–9).

But loving the other person does not stop there. It presses forward to love an unrepentant person enough to rebuke him about his offenses. This topic of rebuking, while clearly biblical, raises a host of tough questions about when to overlook and when to confront someone's offenses. Eight questions can guide us.

Question 1: Is rebuking even an option for a gracious, loving follower of Jesus?

In a culture of tolerance, even the question seems out of place. Nevertheless, this question arises when serious followers of Jesus observe an apparent tension in their Bibles—a common dilemma: Should we overlook someone's sins or should we rebuke the person?

On the one hand, many texts call us to overlook or cover over someone's sins. Consider the following passages:

- "Hatred stirs up dissension, / but love covers over all wrongs" (Prov. 10:12).
- "A fool shows his annoyance at once, / but a prudent man overlooks an insult" (Prov. 12:16).
- "He who covers over an offense promotes love, / but whoever repeats the matter separates close friends" (Prov. 17:9).
- "Starting a quarrel is like breaching a dam; / so drop the matter before a dispute breaks out" (Prov. 17:14).
- "A man's wisdom gives him patience; / it is to his glory to overlook an offense" (Prov. 19:11).

- "Do not resist an evil person. If someone strikes you on the right cheek, turn to him the other also" (Matt. 5:39).
- "Be merciful, just as your Father is merciful" (Luke 6:36; cf. James 2:13).
- "[Love] keeps no record of wrongs" (1 Cor. 13:5).
- "Bear with each other and forgive whatever grievances you may have against one another. Forgive as the Lord forgave you" (Col. 3:13).
- "Above all, love each other deeply, because love covers over a multitude of sins" (1 Pet. 4:8).

In each text, God calls us to overlook or minimize someone's offense. Overlooking, of course, does not mean denial. To overlook means recognizing that a sin has been committed but choosing to forgive that sin attitudinally and to absorb the consequence. To deny means refusing to even evaluate the other person's words or actions. When I overlook your sin, however, I conclude that you have sinned, but I determine to treat you graciously anyway.

On the other hand, many texts call us to confront or rebuke sin:

- "Do not hate your brother in your heart. Rebuke your neighbor frankly so you will not share in his guilt. Do not seek revenge or bear a grudge against one of your people, but love your neighbor as yourself. I am the LORD" (Lev. 19:17–18).
- "Do not rebuke a mocker or he will hate you; / rebuke a wise man and he will love you" (Prov. 9:8).
- "Flog a mocker, and the simple will learn prudence; / rebuke a discerning man, and he will gain knowledge" (Prov. 19:25).
- "Better is open rebuke / than hidden love. / Wounds from a friend can be trusted, / but an enemy multiplies kisses" (Prov. 27:5–6).
- "He who rebukes a man will in the end gain more favor / than he who has a flattering tongue" (Prov. 28:23).
- "You hypocrite, first take the plank out of your own eye, and then you will see clearly to remove the speck from your brother's eye" (Matt. 7:5).
- "If your brother sins against you, go and show him his fault, just between the two of you. If he listens to you, you have won your brother over" (Matt. 18:15).

- "If your brother sins, rebuke him, and if he repents, forgive him. If he sins against you seven times in a day, and seven times comes back to you and says, 'I repent,' forgive him" (Luke 17:3–4).
- "But now I am writing you that you must not associate with anyone who calls himself a brother but is sexually immoral or greedy, an idolater or a slanderer, a drunkard or a swindler. With such a man do not even eat. What business is it of mine to judge those outside the church? Are you not to judge those inside? God will judge those outside. 'Expel the wicked man from among you'" (1 Cor. 5:11–13; also Deut. 17:7; 19:19; 21:21; 22:21, 24; 24:7).
- "Brothers, if someone is caught in a sin, you who are spiritual should restore him gently. But watch yourself, or you also may be tempted. Carry each other's burdens, and in this way you will fulfill the law of Christ" (Gal. 6:1–2).
- "Those who sin are to be rebuked publicly, so that the others may take warning" (1 Tim. 5:20).
- "Warn a divisive person once, and then warn him a second time. After that, have nothing to do with him" (Titus 3:10).
- "My brothers, if one of you should wander from the truth and someone should bring him back, remember this: Whoever turns a sinner from the error of his way will save him from death and cover over a multitude of sins" (James 5:19–20).

What each text in this second list suggests is that God calls us in some sense to confront or rebuke. At the minimum we can conclude that this is an option—even a command—for a Christian to carry out, at least on some occasions.

Question 2: What are the wrong ways to handle the overlook-versus-rebuke dilemma?

If both overlooking and rebuking are legitimate biblical options, then how should we decide which to do in any specific situation? One wrong answer would be to erect ironclad rules, simplistic answers, and unbiblical extremes. These would include "always" or "never" answers: "*Never* confront the person unless . . ." "Raise the issue *every* time someone . . ." Here we might also include cataloging all sins into confrontable versus coverable offenses. Such approaches are too simplistic; they reduce the Bible to a code book.

Another wrong answer to avoid is what others call "devotional theology." Here we make the overlook-versus-rebuke decision based on whatever Bible passage we most recently read. If I read Proverbs 19:11 ("A man's wisdom gives him patience; / it is to his glory to overlook an offense.") this morning, I might be inclined to overlook a coworker's offense. But if I read Proverbs 27:5 ("Better is open rebuke / than hidden love.") the next morning, I might be inclined to confront another coworker who offends me in the same way. Aside from serious questions about how I handle my Bible and apply it to my work life, the impact on my fellow office workers is nothing short of confusing and embarrassing. "These Christians are a weird group. One day they let people walk all over you; the next day they are in your face."

A third wrong response is to procrastinate—to do nothing and hope the conflict somehow resolves itself or fades away. But that's not a biblical option. When an offense occurs, I face a fork in the road. I must choose one path or the other: I must either *confront* the sin or *cover* the sin; I must not *cook* it. I must not allow it to stew in my mind, letting resentment simmer inside. If it is a minor offense, I need to overlook it. If it is a serious offense, I need to rebuke the person. God gives me no middle option of privately holding something against someone.

Question 3: How should we discern when a rebuke is needed?

The rule-of-thumb, default response for Christians should be to overlook offenses. In this way we mirror Jesus, who put up with the many sins of friends and foes throughout his life. "When they hurled their insults at him, he did not retaliate; when he suffered, he made no threats. Instead, he entrusted himself to him who judges justly" (1 Pet. 2:23). "Ah," someone says, "that's fine for Jesus, but I'm not Jesus." But that reply misses the very point of the passage in its context: "To this you were called, because Christ suffered for you, leaving you an example, that you should follow in his steps" (1 Pet. 2:21). Later in the same epistle Peter reminds us that "love covers over a multitude of sins" (1 Pet. 4:8). As one pastor put it, we must learn to throw the blanket of Christian love over the failures of others. Jesus's followers must be marked by patience, long-suffering, and forgiveness (recall chap. 7 above and passages like Gal. 5:22–23; Eph. 4:2–3; Col. 3:12–14).

Yet there are times, as we have seen, when confronting someone is the wisest and most loving course. When should this happen? Seven factors can help us assess each situation.[1]

1. Rebuking might be proper *when the person is trapped in a sin or pattern of sin, or in danger of such.* Galatians 6:1 envisions such a circumstance: "Brothers, if someone is caught in a sin, you who are spiritual should restore him gently." The verb "caught" seemingly means "caught up" or "trapped" in a sin (not "caught red-handed"). In other words, sin entangles, enslaves, and cripples people. When the offender struggles with sins he cannot overcome, then confrontation coupled with counsel, encouragement, or accountability demonstrates Christlike love. True love seeks to rescue trapped sinners; confrontation is one tool God uses to accomplish this.

On other occasions the person might merely appear to be heading down the wrong path. Maybe you have a friend who seems to be forming an improper relationship with someone of the opposite gender. "Kyle, may I share something with you? I'm a bit afraid to bring this up, and I'm not assuming anything wrong or that I know all that might be going on. But it seems to me that you have been getting pretty close to Tanya recently. You seem to spend a lot of time with her on coffee breaks and laugh with her a lot. I guess I'm wondering if there might be something going on. I care about you, Kyle, and about your marriage and reputation at the office." May God give us the boldness to humbly, tentatively, and caringly inquire when we see things that appear unseemly.

2. Rebuking might be proper *when the person may welcome such a rebuke.* Would the offender appreciate and receive your confrontation? Here we encounter another biblical tension that requires humble, prayerful application.

---

[1]Ken Sande, *The Peacemaker: A Biblical Guide to Resolving Personal Conflict*, 3rd ed. (Grand Rapids: Baker, 2004), 150–53, offers four helpful guidelines: An offense is too serious to overlook when it (1) dishonors God, (2) damages your relationship, (3) hurts other people, or (4) hurts the offender. Alfred Poirier, *The Peacemaking Pastor: A Biblical Guide to Resolving Church Conflict* (Grand Rapids: Baker, 2006), 139, suggests two questions: (1) Is the offense a persistent sin, a habitual sin, or the result of bondage to a particular sin? (2) Is the offense hindering my relationship?

> Do not speak to a fool,
>> for he will scorn the wisdom of your words. (Prov. 23:9)

> Do not answer a fool according to his folly,
>> or you will be like him yourself.
> Answer a fool according to his folly,
>> or he will be wise in his own eyes. (Prov. 26:4–5)

The writer of Proverbs calls on us to exercise discernment about the person's openness to be challenged. Likewise, Jesus warns, "Do not give dogs what is sacred; do not throw your pearls to pigs. If you do, they may trample them under their feet, and then turn and tear you to pieces" (Matt. 7:6). We must assess the person's receptivity to the rebuke we think he needs.

3. Rebuking might be proper *when the offense is especially serious, as suggested by the Bible's sin lists.* All sin, of course, is sin, and we must be careful about how we compare one sin with another. Yet certain passages in Scripture suggest that there are levels of severity. Jesus exposes religious leaders who "neglected the more important matters of the law" (Matt. 23:23), and he warns of varying degrees of final punishment (Matt. 11:24; Luke 12:47–48). While we must avoid neatly cataloging sins into coverable versus confrontable offenses, the apostles often cite lists that seem especially heinous and warrant rebuke. Passages like Romans 1:29–31; 1 Corinthians 5:11; 6:9–10; Galatians 5:19–21; Ephesians 5:3–7; Colossians 3:5–11; 1 Peter 4:3; and Revelation 22:15 highlight sins that especially mark the ungodly, invite God's wrath, and must no longer mark God's new people. Among these are various forms of sexual immorality, greed, idolatry, slander, drunkenness, and rage.

4. Rebuking might be proper *when your relationship with someone is severely strained or undermined.* Jesus instructs us, "If your brother sins against you, go and show him his fault, just between the two of you. If he listens to you, you have won your brother over" (Matt. 18:15). Similarly, Jesus counsels in Luke 17:3, "If your brother sins, rebuke him, and if he repents, forgive him." In both texts our Lord addresses unreconciled relationships in which an estranged brother needs to be won back and a repentance-confession dynamic must occur. We are not talking about minor offenses that produce a temporary chill—a

relational glitch—but are forgotten the next day. (My wife and I have had arguments that each of us has forgotten the next day, remembering only that we argued but not remembering the topic.) We are talking about offenses not easily ignored, relational hits that trouble us the next day and bring tension between us.

5. Rebuking might be proper *when the person is hurting himself or jeopardizing his Christian testimony or ministry usefulness.* True love for our neighbor recognizes the self-deceiving, self-destroying nature of sin. That's why Galatians 6:1 calls us to "restore" the person caught in sin. Serious sin problems sideline a believer, rendering him a poor witness for the gospel and a tarnished instrument for helping others.

6. Rebuking might be proper *when others are harmed by the person's sin.* Is the offender's sin harming others? It is one thing for the offender to hurt you, and even to hurt himself. But hurting others is a matter of greater severity. God's call for justice rings out in Proverbs 24:11.

> Rescue those being led away to death;
>   hold back those staggering toward slaughter.

A classic example is gossip. I shamefully remember talking in the church hallway with the wife of a couple I was counseling. Her husband was not a Christian and mistreated her in various ongoing ways. There in the hallway she reported to me and two others her husband's most recent offenses. I said nothing: I merely listened. But that was the problem. The word somehow spread that she was denigrating her husband. He later heard about it and became understandably angry. I had failed to stop her from gossiping.

7. Rebuking might be proper *when the reputation of God, Christ, or his church, or the health or unity of the church, is threatened, injured, or disrupted.* What impact does the offender's sin have on the name of Jesus and on the church's health and unity? In 1 Corinthians 5, the apostle Paul deals with an expression of sexual immorality so evil that it damages the church's reputation and risks infecting the whole body ("a little yeast works through the whole batch of dough," v. 6). Elsewhere, the apostle warns about the disunifying danger of sin: "I urge you, brothers, to watch out for those who cause divisions and put obstacles in your way that are contrary to the teaching you have learned" (Rom. 16:17).

Question 4: What steps of preparation must we take before we seek to rebuke the person?

Let's consider a checklist of essential prerequisites that must be in place before we can effectively confront someone. In addition to meditating on the biblical texts under question 1 above, the following self-examination questions may prove helpful. It may be wise to invite a trusted, mature Christian friend to help you assess your readiness to rebuke.

1. *Have I thoroughly examined my sins and confessed them to God and to the other person I have offended, and have I sought their forgiveness?* Recall our Lord's warnings in Matthew 7:1–5 against sinful judgments (vv. 1–2) and against focusing on the other person's speck while ignoring your planks (vv. 3–5). We must always deal first with our contribution to the relational breakdown before confronting the other person.

2. *Am I forgiving that person attitudinally?* In light of the many passages we examined in chapters 8 and 9, have I entrusted the offender into God's hands, released him from my judgment, dealt with my bitterness (at least initially), and been open to reconcile the relationship if he repents? Internal, heart forgiveness is prerequisite to both confronting the person and granting him transacted forgiveness. This must undergird all our thoughts and dealings toward the other party at every point. Apart from attitudinal forgiveness, my steps of rebuke might proceed with sinful motives.

3. *Do I clearly understand that my goal is to reconcile the relationship and not to defeat an enemy?* The goal of rebuking is not to "show him his fault"—that's the method or means—but to "win" the person (Matt. 18:15). We "rebuke" to draw forth repentance and to transact forgiveness (Luke 17:3). God wants us to "restore him gently" so that we can fulfill the law of Christ (Gal. 6:1). We should minister to the person, not slam-dunk him.

4. *Am I convinced that this is the most loving action I can take?* Do I believe what the Bible teaches above, that rebuke—like a parent's loving discipline—is a display of love? If my conscience is not clear that confronting is an act of love, then I need to delay the step—when in doubt, don't (Rom. 14:23)—until I become convinced by God's Word. We must believe that true love rebukes, even if that seems contrary to our temperament, our parents' example, or our church's climate.

5. *Am I cultivating and expressing the grace attitudes we explored in chapter 7?* As I contemplate rebuking someone, how well am I displaying

the Christlike qualities in passages like Matthew 5:3–12; 1 Corinthians 13:4–7; Galatians 5:22–23; 6:1–2; Ephesians 4:1–3; Colossians 3:12–17; James 3:17–18; and 1 Peter 3:8?

6. *Am I willing to consider the next biblical steps that God might require, if necessary?* Since God does not guarantee that my effort will produce reconciliation, am I willing to follow the path of Matthew 18:15–17 and other passages if the offender hardens himself in response to my rebuke? Am I at least willing to become willing?

7. *Am I seeking to please and fear God more than people?* Am I letting the fear of people cripple me from obeying God and serving as one of his agents to rescue and restore the offender (Gal. 6:1–2; James 5:19–20)?

8. *Do I need some biblical counsel?* Given the challenge and risk that rebuking might bring, it is often helpful to talk it over with someone who can advise, encourage, and pray for you. (Note: There is usually no need to divulge to your advisor the name of the person you need to confront.)

Question 5: What steps should I take to rebuke the person?

Let me suggest a practical procedure for approaching and confronting an offender.

1. *Contact the person privately to express your desire to talk with him privately and face-to-face—either at that time or at a mutually convenient time later.* "John, I'd really like to talk with you about something important, and I wonder if this would be a good time now, or if I can sit down with you later today or tomorrow or sometime soon." It is best for this initial contact to be face-to-face, or at least voice-to-voice (by phone), although if necessary an e-mail or text to set up the meeting can suffice. Our goal is to secure his willingness to talk. The meeting itself, however, should be private and face-to-face. If the person requests someone else to be present (e.g., a spouse), you can seek to understand why and, within reason, accommodate that request.

2. *When you meet with the person, state your concern humbly and tentatively, using "I" messages.* "John, I've been a bit afraid to raise this because I value our relationship, but I'm concerned about something and it's been on my mind. May I share my concern with you?"

3. *Ask about the apparent offense; do not assume and do not accuse.* Even if you have solid evidence of an offense, it is best to start by asking;

160

this gives him opportunity to save face and voluntarily repent. "John, I heard [or saw] something recently and I am wondering if I can ask you about it." Or, "John, I heard you say something the other day that bothered me, and I wasn't sure what to do about it. I may have misunderstood, but I thought I heard you say . . ." A good rule of thumb is "ask, don't assume; ask, don't accuse; just ask." This is especially needful when approaching people in places of God-given authority. We should use extra measures of humility, respect, and charity in light of their position. At the same time, the Bible does not shield leaders from rebuke; none of the passages above exclude leaders from being lovingly approached, and the gravity of their office and their influence on others (recall question 3 above) make the confrontation of their sins even more vital.

4. *Listen to his answer with Christlike compassion and wisdom, and interact wisely with him, with the goal of clearly expressing your concern and inviting him to repent.* Good listening is vital here, as is a gracious attitude that opens the door for his confession and repentance. Our goal is to reflect our seeking Savior, who "came to seek and to save what was lost" (Luke 19:10). We are praying for reconciliation and restoration.

Question 6: What should we do if the person repents and seeks our forgiveness?

In chapter 8 we learned about Cindy, the college freshman betrayed by her boyfriend, Justin, and her best friend, Liz. As we saw, the Lord helped Cindy to forgive Justin attitudinally: to release Justin from her judgment, entrust him to Jesus, deal with her own bitterness, and even make an effort to communicate with him. Unfortunately, Justin chose to pull away completely.

Cindy's relationship with Liz presented a different dynamic. "Justin was a jerk; I get that now," admitted Cindy. "But Liz was my best friend. We're not into the 'BFF' [best friends forever] language, but it was true of us." Unlike Justin, however, Liz was truly broken over what she had done. As soon as Cindy confronted her, Liz confessed. She apologized repeatedly to Cindy, but Cindy was unable to forgive her. As Liz's roommate, she remained civil but silent. But over the course of two or three weeks, as she meditated on the same gospel truths that helped her with Justin, and as she received counsel, support, and encouragement from her pastor's wife, she was able to accept Liz's apology and forgive Liz.

By God's grace, through Cindy and Liz's willingness to pursue peace, he restored their relationship.

How did Cindy respond to Liz's confession? She granted Liz Level 2 transacted forgiveness. Like God, Cindy decided, declared, and promised, because of Jesus, not to raise the matter again—not to herself, to other people, or to Liz. In transacted forgiveness we choose to forgive, we tell the person that we have forgiven him, and we commit to specific promises. Let's consider each of these specific promises and how Cindy expressed them to Liz.

First, in granting someone forgiveness, we promise not to dwell on his sin. "Liz, thank you for confessing your sin. It means a lot to me that you would humble yourself this way and you want to work on our relationship. I want you to know that just as God has forgiven me my massive sin debt through Jesus, so I now forgive you. And I want to explain to you what that means. First, it means that with God's help I will not dwell on your sin. Even if a reminder might flash through my mind, I will remember my commitment before God to not hold your sin against you."

While we cannot promise to never think about it—we can't control the thoughts that enter our minds—we can promise to deal biblically with such thoughts when they do. We can promise not to dwell and brood on the memories. As the old saying goes, you can't stop a bird from landing on your head, but you can stop it from building a nest there. The truths in chapters 8 and 9 are designed to help us shoo birds and prevent nests. Popular notions like "forgive and forget" fall short of a biblical standard because they wrongly assume that we have the capability to somehow erase all memories. The result is ongoing confusion and distorted guilt within people who are not able to simply forget the past.

Second, in granting someone forgiveness, we promise not to mention the matter to others. "Liz, the second promise I am making is not to tell others about your sin. I will seek to protect your reputation and not gossip about you. I'll not tell our dorm friends about this." At the same time, there are two possible exceptions to this no-tell rule: (1) You and the reconciled party might choose to fashion your story into a testimony of God's grace for sharing with others in agreeable ways. But it is vital that the forgiven party feel comfortable about how his past sin might be reported. (2) If you are struggling with ongoing issues related to that person's offense (e.g., haunting memories of his sin, temptations to become bitter), then you might seek biblical counseling from your pastor or another counselor or mature friend. But here your motive should be to deal with your own struggles and not to gossip about the person you have forgiven.

Third, in granting someone forgiveness, we promise not to bring up his sins against him. "Liz, the third promise I am making is to not hold your sins against you or bring them up to hurt you. The past is in the past; we can move forward now. In fact, if I ever bring them up to you, that will be my sin, and I will seek to repent of it and ask your forgiveness." As 1 Corinthians 13:5 says, "[Love] keeps no record of wrongs." It doesn't keep score. This does not mean that there cannot be mutually beneficial dialogue about the sins if the repentant offender is willing; it merely means the forgiving person will not initiate that without permission.

I counseled a couple in which the husband had committed adultery years prior. As I learned about the incident in our first session, they assured me that they had resolved the past, that confession and forgiveness had occurred, and that any current problems were unrelated. But I wondered. In one session they argued back and forth over a seemingly minor matter, blaming each other, until she played the forbidden trump card: "Yeah, but at least I wasn't the one who cheated on you." The discussion ended as he left the room in rage. She sat there with her head in her hands, angry at him but more angry at herself. The past was not properly restored. It took several sessions to unpack the past infidelity and lead them both, for the first time, to true confession, true forgiveness, and true marital unity.

Several corollaries flow from these promises. For example, this means that we must view any repeat sin by the other person as a fresh offense. If love indeed keeps no record of wrongs, then we must not count the number of incidents. Of course, if there is a pattern of sinful behavior, it may be a loving step to express that concern. But to tell the person, "This is the fifth time this month you've done that," calls into question whether we have forgiven him for the previous four occurrences.

Furthermore, making these promises means that, like God, we must bear the consequences of the offender's sins. To use a frequent biblical metaphor for forgiveness, we must absorb the offender's debt and release him from any payment due (see Matt. 6:12, 14–15; 18:21–35). As Miroslav Volf notes, "The heart of forgiveness is a generous release of a genuine debt."[2] To forgive someone requires us to repent of vengeful attitudes that would punish the other person or require him to pay for his sins. Vengeance is not the way God treats us.

Lastly, the promise to forgive means not demanding that the other person change. This might be the most difficult aspect of forgiving someone. While it is reasonable to expect that the person's sincere confession will produce life change, we have no such guarantee, and we must not condition our forgiveness on such a guarantee. I cannot fully know the sincerity of his repentance or the precise level of his commitment; I can only trust God and take the person at his word. Yet even here God is our model. His forgiveness of us does not depend on an assurance that we will never repeat our sins.

In fact, this problem is the number-one obstacle I encounter in counseling someone after a severe betrayal. "I can forgive him for his adultery," says the wife, "but I just need to know that it will never happen again." If you have experienced marriage-ripping betrayal, then perhaps you can relate. It is the most difficult barrier this wife faces. But the problem is that no one can give her an absolute guarantee. Even the most sincerely repentant person who looks his wife in the eye, swears on a stack of Bibles, and means it with all his heart at that moment cannot make an infallible prediction. None of us knows the depth and danger of our remaining sin, not to mention the powerful temptations presented by the Devil and the sinful world around us. Paul's admonition against such arrogance remains true: "So, if you think you are standing firm, be careful that you don't fall!" (1 Cor. 10:12). At the end of the day, the wife must choose to place her trust in her heavenly Father to provide for her, whatever may happen, even if betrayal recurs. Forgiveness carries a cost.

Question 7: What next steps should we take in a forgiven, reconciled relationship?

While Cindy's restored relationship with Liz brought her delight, further steps were needed. For one thing, Cindy gently encouraged Liz to

---

[2]Miroslav Volf, *Free of Charge: Giving and Forgiving in a Culture Stripped of Grace* (Grand Rapids: Zondervan, 2005), 169. Volf, however, does not present the attitudinal-versus-granted distinction, since he is content to assume that God forgives everyone (although he recognizes that not everyone will receive God's forgiveness or ours, and he does urge us to pursue reconciliation).

be sure to address her sin. As true as Liz's repentance and confession before the Lord clearly were, there were dynamics that led Liz to her act of betrayal—matters like her own loneliness, her view of friendship, her understanding of honesty, and so on. In some cases, a reconciled relationship gives us opportunity to suggest to the other party that he or she get some biblical counseling about related issues.

Cindy also needed to address with Liz some lesser concerns that had developed between them. While the betrayal was the major issue, there were lesser matters that needed attention for their relationship to grow. The good news was that Cindy and Liz were now better able to deal with those other struggles. The post-betrayal reconciliation actually deepened their friendship.

With the help of biblical counseling from her pastor's wife, Cindy was able to combat one dangerous mind-set that frequently spoils transacted forgiveness: "I forgive you but I don't want anything to do with you." While this attitude is certainly understandable, especially in response to serious offenses, it is contrary to the grace that God has shown us. The remedy, again, is God's forgiveness. When Cindy's counselor asked, "Aren't you glad—very glad—that God doesn't treat us that way?" Cindy was silent. "Cindy," she continued, "can you imagine God the Father saying to his Son, 'I'm willing to forgive Cindy and let her into my heaven, but I don't want anything to do with her. I know that you died for her, and I will honor our agreement to not condemn her, but in terms of my having any kind of ongoing relationship with her, that's not gonna happen'?" Cindy got the point. True forgiveness seeks to restore the relationship to a wise, appropriate level.[3]

Furthermore, Cindy's path included her occasional need to renew her promises to forgive and to repent of times she violated her promises. If forgiveness is indeed a decision, declaration, and promise that I make to someone, then any violation or reversal of this commitment constitutes sin on my part. Once I promise forgiveness to someone, I cannot renege. If I breach my word by bringing up the person's sin, then I must seek that person's forgiveness. All of this underscores the

---

[3]This does not mean that I need to become friends with someone who raped me, or that I need to abandon all prudent safeguards and precautions that should be present to minimize recurrence. This does not obligate an employer to rehire an employee he justly fired or a church to restore a pastor who repented of adultery. Wisdom, love, propriety, and forgiveness must merge in responding to a repentant offender.

solemnity of forgiving someone. We must not do this hastily. In some cases I ask a counselee to delay announcing his commitment to forgive the other person until the counselee understands the gravity of such a commitment. True forgiveness requires us to count the cost.

Finally, the Lord was calling Cindy and Liz to learn how to love, serve, and minister to each other in new and fresh ways. We will address this in chapter 11.

Question 8: What should we do if the person does not repent and seek our forgiveness?

We will address an unwillingness to repent in chapter 12.

Conclusion

So, how did we do in our effort to reclaim the term *rebuke* as an act of Christ-centered, Spirit-empowered love? The proof will surely come in how well we love the next person in our relational world who needs biblical confrontation.

FOR PERSONAL REFLECTION OR GROUP DISCUSSION

1. What are some reasons why you might be reluctant to confront someone who needs confrontation? Review the Scripture passages under question 1 above, and ask the Lord to give you a heart of love for the other person and a heart that seeks to follow the Lord.

2. Given the high importance the Bible assigns to rebuking, what can you do as an individual church member, and what can your group do as a group, to help normalize the neglected ministry of rebuke and make it more highly valued and more commonly practiced in your church community?

3. Role-play a situation in which one of you must confront someone in the church who has spread gossip about you among your circle of church friends. Then give feedback to the role-play confronter(s), and discuss the best ways to approach someone needing rebuke.

11

Reconciliation in Action

Serving the Other Person

A gentle answer turns away wrath,
but a harsh word stirs up anger.
Proverbs 15:1

Whoever wants to become great among you must be your servant,
and whoever wants to be first must be your slave—
just as the Son of Man did not come to be served,
but to serve, and to give his life as a ransom for many.
Jesus in Matthew 20:26–28

In many ways everything we have seen in the previous chapters is preliminary to the last two. In the first ten chapters we saw how two conflicted parties can exercise mutual repentance and confession before God and each other and receive mutual forgiveness. This, of course, is no small task, and the truths in each chapter have been essential in that process.

But now what? How should I proceed on my end to actually rebuild and advance this relationship now that we have reconciled? That's our focus in this chapter. Chapters 1–10 might occupy the span of several days, weeks, or months; the task outlined in this chapter will engage us for years to come. (The last chapter will address situations where all of the above has failed, and the other party has chosen not to seek reconciliation.)

Let's review the path we have followed to pursue peace. We began with the God of peace, who saves us through the cross, pours out his inner peace on us and into us, promises future worldwide peace, and

The Path for Pursuing Peace
Step 1. Please God
Step 2. Repent
Step 3. Love the person
A. Attitudes of grace
B. Forgive
C. Confront
D. Serve

calls and enables us to pursue relational peace with everyone in our path (chap. 1). We also donned biblical glasses to view conflict God's way: conflicts are inevitable, therefore expect them; sinful, therefore resolve them; and opportunities, therefore seize them (chap. 2). We then began walking down the peacemaking path, starting with Step 1, the commitment to please God in response to his grace (chap. 3). Next, we unpacked Step 2, the step of identifying, repenting of, and confessing both our heart and behavior sins before both God and others (chaps. 4–6). With chapter 7 we began Step 3, exploring some key attitudes of grace needed in our relationships. We then focused on the key attitude of forgiveness, addressing forgiveness on both the attitudinal and granted levels (chaps. 8–9). And in chapter 10 we considered how and when to confront the other person and to grant transacted forgiveness.

Assuming we have achieved reconciliation, we need to explore what ongoing love looks like. The same Christlike love that leads us to display gracious attitudes, forgive from the heart, rebuke as needed, and forgive transactionally must continue to guide us after reconciliation occurs. How do I conserve the positive energy and momentum that God's Spirit has brought to us and move forward to experience all the peace that Jesus died and rose to secure between me and my brother or sister?

The key word in this chapter is to *serve* the other person. We love others by serving them in Christlike ways.

Serving Others Like Jesus Did

We begin with Jesus. Mark 10 records an incident of conflict among Jesus's twelve disciples near the end of his earthly ministry, as opposition against him increased. James and John come to Jesus with a specific demand: "Teacher," they say, "we want you to do for us whatever we ask.... Let one of us sit at your right and the other at your left in your glory" (vv. 35–37). Jesus responds to them with a direct and sobering challenge about the severe cost of following him and the fact that final placement in the kingdom is not his decision (vv. 38–40). The first (right-hand) and second (left-hand) highest places at the final messianic banquet (or on the thrones of final judgment) are not up for grabs.

Ideally, the matter would end right there with this gentle rebuke from Jesus to this pair of brothers. But it gets worse: "When the ten heard about this, they became indignant with James and John" (v. 41). Sadly, this is not the first time we witness interpersonal conflict among these close followers of Jesus. Judging from Jesus's response, their indignation stems from pride, jealousy, and arrogance, and is far from righteous anger. And so Jesus issues a manifesto.

> Jesus called them together and said, "You know that those who are regarded as rulers of the Gentiles lord it over them, and their high officials exercise authority over them. Not so with you. Instead, whoever wants to become great among you must be your servant, and whoever wants to be first must be slave of all. (Mark 10:42–44)

What is our Lord's answer to conflict among his followers? A heart marked by servanthood. Contrary to the world's notions of greatness as ruling over others and enslaving them to serve us, Jesus declares that true greatness involves serving others. He uses the synonymous images of servants and slaves to show the humble depth of this lifestyle, and he extends the call to include serving anyone and everyone. In James and John's wrangling over placement in the kingdom, and in the other ten's sinful response, they look too much like ungodly leaders.

Jesus then brings a striking climax to his appeal: "For even the Son of Man did not come to be served, but to serve, and to give his life as a ransom for many" (Mark 10:45). Our Lord's own sacrificial death provides the ultimate example of service. Alluding to Isaiah 53, Jesus sees himself as the suffering servant and his imminent death as providing a ransom—a payment to release his people from their captivity and to make us God's own possession. But he is more than our Redeemer in this passage. He is our model—our perfect example—of serving others.[1] Moved and empowered by the Redeemer, we pursue a life of service and reject the self-centeredness that inevitably breeds conflict.

---

[1] Good theologians are fond of extracting key truths about Jesus and his saving work from verses like Mark 10:45; Eph. 5:2; and Phil. 2:5–8, to highlight vital aspects of Jesus's death. But better theologians—who concur with those insights but are sensitive to the

Having reconciled with the other person, how do we serve him and how do we strengthen that relationship? Three ministry strategies are vital to promoting relational growth.

Ministry Strategy 1: Know the Person

First, get to know the other person and his tendencies, personality, attitudes so you can serve that person wisely and sensitively. One mark of wise relational ministry is treating people as individuals. The apostle Paul understood this aim: "Remember that for three years I never stopped warning *each of you* night and day with tears" (Acts 20:31). "We proclaim him, admonishing and teaching *everyone* with all wisdom, so that we may present *everyone* perfect in Christ" (Col. 1:28). "We worked night and day in order not to be a burden to *anyone* while we preached the gospel of God to you. . . . For you know that we dealt with *each of you* as a father deals with his own children" (1 Thess. 2:9, 11).

Consider, for example, Paul's variety of ministry strategies in 1 Thessalonians 5:14: "And we urge you, brothers, warn those who are idle, encourage the timid, help the weak, be patient with everyone." The apostle is not erecting a threefold scientific personality typology, three distinguishable categories into which we can place each human. Instead, he encourages his readers to minister in tailored ways to specific kinds of people—different strokes for different folks. Table 2 illustrates the distinctions Paul makes. Note the three distinct descriptions and the three corresponding distinct ministry actions.

Table 2. Differing ministries to different kinds of people

Description of the Person (Noun)	Ministry Action (Verb)
Idle (NIV, ESV), unruly (NASB)	Warn (NIV, ESV), admonish (NASB)
Timid (NIV, ESV), fainthearted (NASB)	Encourage (NIV, ESV, NASB)
Weak (NIV, ESV, NASB)	Help (NIV, ESV, NASB)

The first category pictures someone who is lazy, undisciplined, or slack and who needs to be admonished to work, per Paul's example (1 Thess. 2:9), command (4:11), and warning (2 Thess. 3:6–16). The

---

contextual flow of the passages—realize that the writer's main point in these passages is not about Jesus's cross but about his call to radical service (Mark 10:43–45), radical love (Eph. 5:1–2; cf. 5:25–27), and radical others-centeredness (Phil. 2:1–11), with his death being presented as the definitive display of that specific relational grace enjoined upon us.

second suggests someone who is fearful or discouraged and who needs encouragement and strength. The timidity could be temperamental, or it could be occasioned by hard circumstances (e.g., persecution, spiritual doubts, fears about the plight of their deceased Christian friends, etc. in 1 Thessalonians). The last category might refer to someone who is physically weak or sickly (1 Cor. 11:30; James 5:13–16); positionally weak, lowly, or uninfluential (1 Cor. 1:27; 12:22); or spiritually weak, someone with a weak conscience or easily tempted (Rom. 14:1; 15:1; 1 Cor. 8:7–10; 9:22; Gal. 4:9). This person needs to be helped and supported in appropriate ways. First Thessalonians 5:14 ends by adding that patience must mark each of these interactions.

How do these truths play out in reconciling a conflicted relationship? One way is by charitably not assuming the worst motives behind someone's offending action. I can more easily forgive someone when I recognize that his failure might have arisen from fear or ignorance more than malice. When Scott's wife Tara disagrees, in front of the children, with Scott's disciplinary measures, it may have more to do with fear than rebellion—she fears that the children will become angry. As she and Scott work through this parenting conflict, he might find it wiser to encourage his timid wife than to admonish her. Likewise, Tara might discover that Scott's questionable disciplinary steps stem more from ignorance, inexperience, or naiveté than from harshness. She might assist him most by providing advice from her motherly perspective or suggesting people or resources to assist them as parents.

Ministry Strategy 2: Godly Listening and Godly Speaking

One indispensable skill set that underlies the ministry strategy above and below is Christ-centered communication. Good communication can lubricate every conflicted relationship, whether the parties reconcile or remain unreconciled.

What does godly listening involve? Three lines of biblical truth about listening will help us rebuild our relationship with someone we have had (or still have) conflict with. First, God himself is our perfect model of listening. The three persons within the Godhead listen to each other. God the Father listens to his Son (John 11:41–42) and to the Spirit (Rom. 8:26–27), God the Son listens to his Father (John 8:26; 14:24), and God the Holy Spirit listens to both the Father and the Son (John 16:13).

Second, God listens to us, his people (Gen. 16:7–16; Ex. 2:23–25; Isa. 59:1; 1 Pet. 3:12). Perhaps the most touching picture of God's listening grace comes in Genesis 16. Mistreated by her mistress, the Egyptian slave Hagar flees Sarai and Abram and begins to head home. But God intervenes: "The angel of the LORD found Hagar near a spring in the desert" and he spoke to her (vv. 7–8). In verse 11 we read about the God who hears.

> The angel of the LORD also said to her:
>
> > "You are now with child
> >   and you will have a son.
> > You shall name him Ishmael [meaning God hears],
> >   for the LORD has heard of your misery."

God finds her, speaks to her, hears her, and sees her ("'You are the God who sees me,' for she said, 'I have now seen the One who sees me,'" v. 13).

If Genesis 16 is the most moving story, perhaps Exodus 2 is the most powerful.

> During that long period, the king of Egypt died. The Israelites groaned in their slavery and cried out, and their cry for help because of their slavery went up to God. God heard their groaning and he remembered his covenant with Abraham, with Isaac and with Jacob. So God looked on the Israelites and was concerned about them. (Ex. 2:23–25; also 3:7–10)

The inspired writer connects God's hearing of his suffering people with his covenantal remembering. And in the very next chapter the Lord acts, appearing to Moses and launching the plan to rescue Israel from Egypt. Salvation begins with the ears of God, as Isaiah 59:1 also affirms:

> Surely the arm of the LORD is not too short to save,
>   nor his ear too dull to hear.

Our Redeemer is all ears.

That leads to the third truth about listening. God calls us to listen to others in similar ways. Let Dietrich Bonhoeffer's classic work *Life Together* bridge God's listening and ours: "But Christians have forgotten that the ministry of listening has been committed to them by Him who is Himself the great listener and whose work they should share."[2]

What should mark Godlike listening to others? For one thing, God calls us to listen actively and attentively—to be engaged, to give eye contact, to labor to understand what the person says, not just put up with their ramblings. Proverbs 18:13 declares,

> He who answers before listening—
>   that is his folly and his shame.

James 1:19 reminds us that "everyone should be quick to listen, slow to speak and slow to become angry." In addition, godly listening is also caring and compassionate, like God's listening in Genesis 16 and Exodus 2 above. Christlike listeners seek to emulate Paul's descriptions in Romans 12:15, "Rejoice with those who rejoice; mourn with those who mourn," and 1 Corinthians 12:26, "If one part suffers, every part suffers with it; if one part is honored, every part rejoices with it." As one writer has put it, "A true friend is one who cares enough to hear the things that remain unspoken."

During a session of marital mediation with a separated couple, James told Renee about a recent conversation he had with their middle-school son while the son was visiting him. The boy had made a comment about drugs, and the husband proceeded to talk to him about the dangers of drugs, including information about what kind of drugs are out there, how they are used, people he knew who had died from overdosing, and how he had regretfully used drugs when he was younger. I was encouraged by his fatherly care and boldness, though I said nothing. But Renee was angry. "I wish you had told me that you had that conversation," she sharply told her husband. "I have a right to know about those kinds of talks, and I wish you had told me what he said; and I wish you had talked to me before you told him all that."

As I reflected on that interchange I sympathized with the mom. She had sought to follow Jesus in the marriage, and he had not. She was the primary custodial parent in their agreement. She understandably would want to know about her son's comment and her

---

[2]Dietrich Bonhoeffer, *Life Together: The Classic Exploration of Faith in Community*, trans. John W. Doberstein (New York: HarperCollins, 1954), 98–99.

separated husband's speech. Yet I was also sad about the opportunity she missed to love her alienated husband with compassionate ears. How wonderful would it have been for her to respond, "James, thank you for spending time with our son, for caring about his temptations, and for being willing to give him some honest counsel, even to share some shameful details about your own past. Thank you for doing that. I would appreciate knowing about it the next time you have that kind of conversation with our son, so please be sure to tell me, but do know that I'm glad you had that talk." In our private follow-up, Renee regretted her response. She later apologized to James, expressed the wiser words I suggested above, and emerged from this as a more Christlike listener.

What does godly speaking involve? In response to God's saving grace (Eph. 4:1, 20–24), we can draw four marks about godly speech from Ephesians 4:25–5:2. First, our words should be *honest*: "Therefore each of you must put off falsehood and speak truthfully to his neighbor, for we are all members of one body" (Eph. 4:25). As the writer of Proverbs puts it,

> An honest answer
> is like a kiss on the lips. (Prov. 24:26)

How can I open myself in wise, transparent ways to the person I am seeking to serve?

Second, our words should be *beneficial*: "Do not let any unwholesome talk come out of your mouths, but only what is helpful for building others up according to their needs, that it may benefit those who listen" (Eph. 4:29). Unwholesome words must not be limited to cuss words, but are any words that tear down and fall short of edifying speech.

> Reckless words pierce like a sword,
> but the tongue of the wise brings healing. (Prov. 12:18)

What words will best minister to the other person? What words will refresh and nourish my friends and family members, especially those with whom I have had conflict?

Third, our words should be *timely*. As we saw in Ephesians 4:29 above, Paul urges words that will build others up "according to their needs," or better translated, "as fits the occasion" (ESV).

> A man finds joy in giving an apt reply—
> and how good is a timely word! (Prov. 15:23)

What words will best minister to this person at this time? What words are fitting right now? Rebuilding a reconciled relationship sometimes requires wise timing, especially if the other party struggles with forgiving us.

Fourth, our words should be *kind*. "Get rid of all bitterness, rage and anger, brawling and slander, along with every form of malice. Be kind and compassionate to one another, forgiving each other, just as in Christ God forgave you" (Eph. 4:31–32).

> A gentle answer turns away wrath,
> but a harsh word stirs up anger. (Prov. 15:1)

What words and tones will best convey Christlike kindness? How can I frame my responses to reflect compassion and grace?

Ministry Strategy 3: Work Together with Mutual Understanding to Solve Problems

Even when we are able to reconcile a relationship with someone, differences of opinion on important issues often remain. Perhaps you serve on a ministry team in your church that is tasked by the leaders to research and recommend the best Sunday school curriculum. During one of the meetings you and another team member disagree about something, and things get a bit heated. You both speak rudely to each other, and one of you walks out of the meeting. God then convicts you both of your sin and leads you to pursue peace. You reconcile your relationship through mutual confession and forgiveness. All is done, right? No! Which curriculum will you use? The original difference of opinion about the curriculum—the occasion for the now-reconciled relational conflict—remains unresolved. Likewise, if a husband and wife exchange unkind words in a conversation about school choices for their children, they need to repent of their sinful words and reconcile their relationship, as we have seen in the first ten chapters. But they still need to decide what school their kids will attend.

How should we settle material or substantive questions—decisions that need to be made, actions that need to be chosen, or products that need to be purchased?

Although we began this book by looking at the peacemaking theme in Romans, my favorite peacemaking book is Philippians. People popularly summarize its theme as joy, but that seems to be a by-product of a larger theme: unity for the sake of the gospel (based on 1:27–28; also 2:2–4 and 4:2–3). Philippians 2 in particular paints a powerful picture of radical others-centeredness. Paul begins in verse 1 by summarizing five descriptors of the salvation we have in Christ: "If you have any encouragement from being united with Christ, if any comfort from his love, if any fellowship with the Spirit, if any tenderness and compassion . . ." The "if" that begins each phrase is a "logical if" (used in an argument), an "if" that carries the sense of "since." While the first three terms explicitly reference Jesus and his Spirit, the last two terms, "tenderness" and "compassion," also point to God's saving work. The Greek translation of the Old Testament (the Septuagint) uses this language to describe God's saving grace toward his people Israel. All five of the descriptors summarize God's salvation work in us.

Based on God's grace provisions and our identity as his saved people in verse 1 ("If you have . . ."), Paul exhorts us in verses 2–4 to pursue relational like-mindedness and radical others-centeredness.

> . . . then make my joy complete by being like-minded, having the same love, being one in spirit and purpose. Do nothing out of selfish ambition or vain conceit, but in humility consider others better than yourselves. Each of you should look not only to your own interests, but also to the interests of others. (Phil. 2:2–4)

Paul's central goal of unity in verse 2 is plain: "being like-minded, having the same love, being one in spirit and purpose." The language echoes the vision of Philippians 1:27: "I will know that you stand firm in one spirit, contending as one man for the faith of the gospel." For this unity to emerge, the readers must avoid self-centeredness and practice radical others-centeredness (2:3–4; see further below).

In the rest of chapter 2 the apostle presents four examples of radical others-centeredness. Verses 5–11 highlight the greatest example, our Lord Jesus. As our model (v. 5), Jesus passed through several steps of humiliation in leaving heaven, becoming human, and letting himself be killed, even through the shameful death of crucifixion (vv. 6–8).[3] But Jesus is not the only one who embodies this sacrificial love for others. In verses 17–18, Paul testifies of his own self-sacrificial ministry of "being poured out like a drink offering." Verses 19–24 describe Timothy as one "who takes a genuine interest in your welfare. For everyone looks out for his own interests, not those of Jesus Christ," words strikingly similar to verses 2–4 above. And verses 25–30 recall Epaphroditus, the messenger and gift bearer the Philippians sent to Paul. Apparently Epaphroditus was near death because of illness. Yet verse 26 reports his distress—not because he was sick, but because *they heard* about his illness. So others-centered was Epaphroditus that he was more concerned about the Philippians' response to his illness than about his own health!

A Problem-Solving Tool

Todd and Katie had been married twelve years and recently hit a brick wall in planning their summer vacation week. Todd wanted to go with Katie and their two preteen children to Virginia Beach; Katie wanted them all to visit both sets of grandparents in Pittsburgh. Sadly, things heated up every time they broached the subject. They accused each other of being selfish, uncaring, and insensitive, and their various rounds of negotiation always ended with tears or rage, followed by twenty-four-hour periods of coldness and distance. Finally, they shared the conflict with Gary, their small-group leader. He wisely understood that God's first priority for Katie and Todd was to reconcile their sinful arguments. Gary led them through the steps we saw in previous chapters. They recalibrated their focus on pleasing God, they confessed their sinful speech, and they sought and received each other's forgiveness. But they still needed to decide their vacation plans.

---

[3]Rather than viewing this passage primarily as a proof text for the doctrine of Jesus's incarnation, death, resurrection, and ascension, better exegetes understand Philippians 2 to be Paul's call for radical others-centeredness, in which Jesus serves as the example par excellence to persuade the reader to obey 2:3-4.

One helpful decision-making technique for parties with differing opinions is Ken Sande's Issue-Position-Interests model.[4] Let me picture Sande's concept with a diagram (fig. 6) that summarizes their discussion.

Figure 6. The Issue-Position-Interests model

Issue:

Position A: Position B:

Interests: Interests:

Goal: Agreed Position:

In this approach, an issue is a specific, concrete decision to make or a question to answer. A position is the preferred decision or answer that one party brings to the discussion. And interests are the reasons, arguments, or motives that support the position held by each party.

The art of successful resolution of these matters involves sensitively understanding and humbly seeking to capture the other person's interest in a mutually satisfying outcome. This goal is higher than mere compromise or alternating which party gets his way over time. For Christians, our goal comes from Philippians 2:4: "Each of you should look not only to your own interests, but also to the interests of others." As we saw in our Philippians summary above, considering the interests of others (along with the other calls to like-mindedness and others-centeredness in vv. 2–4) flows from the salvation provisions God has given us in verse 1 and is exemplified by Jesus, Paul, Timothy, and Epaphroditus in verses 5–30.

How did Todd and Katie work through this issue in a way that pleased God and reflected mutual understanding and marital peace? First, they clarified the question. One of Katie's replies to Todd's desire to go to the beach, in her argument to visit their in-laws, was that she didn't like the beach. Gary helped them redefine the issue: "Should we visit our relatives or should we do a private family vacation (that could

---

[4]Ken Sande, *The Peacemaker: A Biblical Guide to Resolving Personal Conflict*, 3rd ed. (Grand Rapids: Baker, 2004), chap. 11.

mean the beach but could also mean the mountains or sightseeing in Washington, DC, to be discussed and decided later)?"[5]

How did Gary help Katie and Todd work through these issues with the I.P.I. diagram (see fig. 7)? He began by reading and reminding them of Philippians 2:1–4 and both their identity in Christ and the Lord's call for them to be radically others-centered. They prayed together and asked the Lord to give them Philippians 2 hearts. They also read aloud Romans 12:10: "Be devoted to one another in brotherly love. Honor one another above yourselves."

Figure 7. The Issue-Position-Interests model applied

Issue: Visit in-laws or do a private family vacation?	
Position A: Private family vacation (Todd)	**Position B:** Visit in-laws (Katie)
Interests:	**Interests:**
I want a private vacation with just us four. I'm not relaxed around my parents and in-laws. Our own vacation is a good way to make memories. We visit in-laws every Christmas already.	Our parents are getting older, and they may not be around much longer. Visiting in-laws is a good way to make memories. It would save money; summer rentals are expensive.
Goal: Agreed Position: A or B or a new option C?	

Gary then asked Todd to allow Katie to summarize her position and interests without interruption, with the single goal of Todd trying charitably, compassionately, and appreciatively to understand her. Katie then shared her position and interests. Gary then asked Todd to speak to Katie and summarize what he heard Katie share with him, without criticizing or dismissing her or defending his view. Gary asked Katie to comment on whether Todd had indeed understood her. While there were a few aspects Todd didn't initially catch—some follow-up dialogue brought clarification—Gary's ministry goal was reached: for the first

---

[5] A related prior question could also have been introduced: Should we travel at all, or might we find it more profitable as a family to stay home for a week and do a few day trips, restaurant splurges, and an at-home family project? In this case, both Todd and Katie readily preferred to travel somewhere.

time, Todd truly understood Katie's thinking and Katie felt understood. Gary then reversed the process and asked Todd to share his position and interests and for Katie then to listen and summarize. And for the first time, Katie understood Todd, and Todd felt understood by Katie.

Todd and Katie later reported that the time invested in mutual understanding was the best thirty minutes they had spent with each other in a long time. Todd was moved by the evident love Katie showed for his mom and dad and her desire to see their children develop deepening relationships with both sets of in-laws. Katie, who had prejudged Todd's motives for not wanting to visit their relatives, was encouraged by Todd's sincere desire for them to connect with each other as a foursome on a special family vacation. She had also underestimated the work pressures Todd was facing; she knew that visiting their parents would not meet his longing for a relaxing time away.

As both Katie and Todd sought to understand and prefer one another, another desired result emerged: they began to adopt and even own each other's interests. Todd wanted Katie and the kids to connect with the kids' grandparents; Katie wanted some foursome time with just their family and wanted Todd to get some true rest and relaxation. As they talked further, Gary encouraged them to pray, thanking God for giving them mutual compassion and asking God to help them make a wise decision.

The decision Todd and Katie happened to reach is somewhat incidental to this book. My main goal has been to encourage readers to adopt the Christ-centered goals and communication process outlined above. But I am also happy to report the decision. They decided that they would visit their extended family in Pittsburgh for three days and then spend three more days at a mountain and lake retreat area in West Virginia. In fact, so much did they seek to look out for each other's interests that they ended up advocating the other person's original position ("Todd, we can visit our in-laws another time!" "Katie, our folks are getting older!") and came close to creating a new argument! In terms of their marital maturation, whatever family memories the vacation brought were far less important than the memories they gained from working through this decision in God-delighting ways.

Not every decision, however, can allow two people to blend their respective desires. In some situations, a compromise is not possible—we must do A or B and can't merge them into a new option C as Todd and Katie did. However, by compassionately understanding each other's interests and seeking by God's grace to prefer one another, two parties can together select A or B—not with an "I win, you lose" attitude, but with a united sense that A or B would be the wisest joint decision to make.

Conclusion

As we saw at the start of this chapter, the call to serve one another that is so vital to any relationship comes from Jesus our Redeemer, the one who "did not come to be served, but to serve, and to give his life as a ransom for many" (Mark 10:45). This Savior not only provides the ransom payment for our sins and perfectly models radical others-centeredness, but also promises us his power to help: "I can do everything through him who gives me strength" (Phil. 4:13). He alone can forgive and change you; only his grace can pardon and empower. If you belong to Jesus, then this Redeemer has freed you from the captivity, enslavement, and condemnation that once marked your life, and he can enable you today to serve those with whom you have had conflict.

FOR PERSONAL REFLECTION OR GROUP DISCUSSION

1. Memorize and meditate on Mark 10:45 as a foundational verse to rivet your eyes on Jesus and to give you a service agenda for every relationship. How does Jesus Christ as your Redeemer help you in your daily relationships?

2. Describe a situation in which the Issue-Position-Interests model might shed light on two different sets of competing interests by two parties in conflict. (Consider various friendship, family, work, or church relationships.) Then discuss how understanding and appreciating interests might lead to an agreeable solution between the parties.

3. Review the above biblical truths about Christlike communication. What specific marks of godly listening and godly speaking do you need to work on and pray about? For a helpful Bible study on godly speech, study Proverbs 10 and 12, the two most compact chapters in Proverbs on the tongue. Latch on to a few key verses there that can guide you in your daily relationships.

12

When Nothing Works

Loving Enemies and Those Who Act Like Them

Christians who take vengeance into their own hands strap on the six guns,
coil up their rope, and ride off into the sunset as truly as did
the vigilantes on the frontier. . . . Loosen that belt, untie the cord
around your right leg, let the guns fall off
as you sink to your God in repentance.

Jay E. Adams

But I tell you who hear me: Love your enemies, do good to those who hate you,
bless those who curse you, pray for those who mistreat you.

Jesus in Luke 6:27–28

I wish this chapter were not needed. It's the saddest part of the book. Yet for some of us it is indispensable. It seeks to answer a simple question: What if the steps for pursuing peace don't work? What if our efforts fail to achieve reconciliation? What if the other person remains hostile, cold, or irreconcilable? Maybe you have no such alienated relationships. But your friends do, and they need your help. "I've been doing what you told me to do," declares your frustrated friend after her recent separation, "but it doesn't seem to be working. He's still not willing to work on anything related to our marriage or even to return my phone calls." "I'm

> ### The Path for Pursuing Peace
> Step 1. Please God
> Step 2. Repent
> **Step 3. Love the person**
>   A. Attitudes of grace
>   B. Forgive
>   C. Confront
>   **D. Serve (continued)**

done trying to deal with this relationship; we need to find another church." No small part of my nearly thirty years of pastoral ministry has been given to helping counselees deal with difficult people.

In chapter 11 we developed three ministry strategies to strengthen a reconciled relationship. Five ministry strategies can help us deal with people who will not reconcile with us.[1]

Ministry Strategy 1: Keep Your Relationship with God Central

Two Bible truths about our relationship to God are vital when we deal with those who harden themselves against our peacemaking efforts. First, we must supremely cherish our identity in Christ and our acceptance by the Father. Consider Psalm 27:10.

> Though my father and mother forsake me,
>   the LORD will receive me.

Whether the forsaking party is a parent, spouse, boss, or close friend, the psalmist models a life-changing perspective: our acceptance by God takes priority over our acceptance by others. The unseen reality of a God who embraces us outweighs the seen reality of human rejection. One helpful activity to reinforce God's love is to review the Bible passages we discussed in chapter 8 (especially the "Pictures of God's Forgiveness") and chapter 9 (the six gospel facts designed to combat bitterness). By studying, memorizing, and praying over these truths we will deepen our roots in the Lord who receives us. God's reception of us can trump our despair over other damaged relationships.

Second, we must keep our eyes on pleasing God. Pursuing peace in godly ways does not guarantee that the other person will reciprocate and seek reconciliation. After all, the perfect Peacemaker was brutally killed. Yet Jesus understood that pleasing his Father was his highest aim in life. Even his supreme display of horizontal love for his people—the cross— was not done apart from this God-pleasing motive: "Be imitators of God,

---

[1] Let me also recommend two Christ-centered resources along these lines: Jay E. Adams, *How to Overcome Evil: An Exposition of Romans 12:14–21* (Phillipsburg, NJ: Presbyterian and Reformed, 1977); and Ken Sande, *The Peacemaker: A Biblical Guide to Resolving Personal Conflict*, 3rd ed. (Grand Rapids: Baker, 2004), chap. 12, in which Sande presents five strategies based on Rom. 12:14–21: (1) Control your tongue. (2) Seek godly advisors. (3) Keep doing what is right. (4) Recognize your limits. (5) Use the ultimate weapon: love.

therefore, as dearly loved children and live a life of love, just as Christ loved us and gave himself up for us as a fragrant offering and sacrifice to God" (Eph. 5:1–2). The apostle reminds us that Jesus did not die for *our sake* only but also for *his Father*, to bring him delight by offering a sweet-smelling sacrifice. In the same way, we might not achieve reconciliation with others, but we can please God and hear his commendation, "Well done, good and faithful servant." I regularly encourage couples to love their spouses not because they deserve it—your husband didn't climb up on the cross to die for you—but because your Lord Jesus deserves it. I encourage the wife to visualize by faith Jesus standing above and behind her husband, and to love and serve her husband with her eyes on Jesus. When she does that, none of her love and service toward her husband, even if he never reciprocates, is ever wasted. Her God will reward her. "God is not unjust; he will not forget your work and the love you have shown *him* as you have helped his people and continue to help them" (Heb. 6:10).

Ministry Strategy 2: Review, Renew, and Redo Your Personal Peacemaking Efforts

When we find the other person to be unresponsive, we are tempted to give up. Instead, the Lord wants us to review our commitment to please God, and redo any of the above steps that need redoing. Ask yourself questions like these:

- Has pleasing God been my highest desire? Where do I need to adjust my goals in relationship to him?
- Have I examined and repented of any ways I have sinned against this person? Have I humbled myself before him?
- Do I need an attitude adjustment by God's Spirit? Am I harboring any resentment or bitterness in my heart?
- Do I need to allow more time?

In considering these things, seek counsel from a pastor or biblical counselor. If it's a matter of the other person not forgiving you for your previously confessed sin, then review chapter 6. If it's a matter of the other person's unwillingness to deal with his sin, then review chapter 8. Either way, a second or third approach seems warranted. If these efforts still fail, you may need to appeal to him to let you invite a third-party facilitator to assist you both. If the person remains resistant, you may need to bring in others to help (Matt. 18:15–17). While his agreement to do this would be ideal, it is not required; you unilaterally can invite a third party. Of course it is vital that you proceed carefully here and that you get sound biblical counsel.[2]

Ministry Strategy 3: Seek Help

Given the high importance Jesus and his apostles assign to reconciliation (recall chap. 2), seeking help is wise. Don't do this alone. Enlist the help of others. What kind of help should you consider? Let me suggest three avenues.

First, seek godly counsel and personal accountability on how to handle whatever frustrations you feel and how to proceed in this relationship (including applying the other steps in this chapter). Ask a pastor, biblical counselor, or mature Christian friend to help you. That person can counsel you and can perhaps serve as a third-party facilitator. As a pastor, I regularly minister in both ways to members facing conflict. Ask this person (or these persons) to encourage you, pray for you, and provide loving accountability through this growth process. Share openly your story, seeking to be honest in your assessment and to not malign the other party. Along with sharing the facts of the situation and your emotional struggles, describe the efforts you have made to reconcile so this person can best support you, challenge you, and guide you.

A second form of help that you might seek is temporal assistance— financial aid, legal advice, childcare support, medical care, employment assistance, and the like. If you have sought church-based counseling, then your pastor or church leader can connect you to resources within the church. Your church might have a benevolence fund to help members with various financial hardships (e.g., if the unreconciled relationship involves a spouse who has left you or a boss who has fired you). You might also find governmental or community-based resources that can guide you and provide various benefits and services.

Third, in some cases, you may need to seek justice or financial protection for you and your family through church or civil authorities. If the offender is part of your church, then you can approach your

---

[2]For further help in dealing with matters of restorative church discipline, see Jay E. Adams, *Handbook for Church Discipline* (Grand Rapids: Zondervan, 1986), and Sande, *The Peacemaker*, chap. 9.

church leaders to ask them to redress the problem. Churches that follow the biblical practice of restorative church discipline can help both the offender and the offended to find just solutions to their problems. Church discipline brings the loving pressure of the entire body of Christ to help the offender repent (see Matt. 18:15–20; 1 Corinthians 5; etc.). While 1 Corinthians 6:1–7 prohibits Christians from suing Christians, the same passage envisions the Lord's provision—the local church serving its members by providing conflict coaching, mediation, and arbitration to assist believers to resolve substantive conflicts without litigation. If the offender is not a Christian or if he rejects the church's authority, then civil court actions might be needed to obtain justice and financial protection.[3]

On the other hand, if he has physically harmed you or engaged in criminal actions that endanger you or your family (e.g., domestic violence, theft, kidnapping your child, drug or illegal activities that expose you and your family to danger), you need to call the police. God has provided civil authority in Romans 13:1–6 to protect citizens from evildoers. The prohibition against taking personal revenge in Romans 12:17–21 also calls us to leave room for God's judgment—a judgment that includes the government as God's agent for justice and punishment in Romans 13:1–6 (compare 12:19 with 13:4). If the person cannot govern himself, he needs to be governed by others. The most loving action in some cases—what's best for the offender's soul—may be for him to be bodily incarcerated. While God has not given his church the authority to punish evildoers, the church has an overlapping jurisdiction before God to shepherd its members, even if they face criminal charges or imprisonment.

Of course, in any pursuit of judicial or police help, the Christian should seek to demonstrate Christlikeness in dealing with others. Even if calling the police may be right in certain situations (e.g., domestic violence), the believer should live by faith—not fear—trusting God to care for you. And such a call should proceed not from revenge or rage but from true love for the offender, a love that sees the offender's need for his destructive behavior to be arrested.

---

[3]If you have been threatened with a lawsuit or are contemplating filing one, I recommend appendix D in Sande, *The Peacemaker*, 279–86. For resources and training to help your church cultivate a culture of peace and handle conflict biblically, contact Peacemaker Ministries (www.peacemaker.net).

Ministry Strategy 4: Frame and Follow a Practical, Christ-centered, Ongoing Plan to Minister to the Other Party

Some unreconciled relationships fade away with time. We lose touch with that former friend. We quit or get fired from the job and no longer see that unrepentant boss or coworker. We finish the school year, change degree programs, or graduate. In chapter 8, Cindy faced this situation with Justin, the three-month boyfriend who betrayed her and later transferred to another school. Such relationships are temporary.

But other unreconciled relationships don't fade, nor should they. Maybe it's a family member, church member, close friend, spouse, or ex-spouse who remains a co-parent. How should we handle such a relationship that is distant or hostile? Ideally, three characteristics should mark our ministry plan: (1) It must be practical, one that includes specific, concrete, doable steps. (2) It must be a long-term, ongoing plan—not a quick-fix, flash-in-the-pan effort but a lifestyle of persevering love. (Since we have no basis for assuming the person will change, be prepared for a long-term ministry.) (3) And it must reflect the teaching and example of Jesus and his apostles.

I know of no better starting place than Luke 6:27–36, a passage in which Jesus teaches his followers how to love their enemies.

> But I tell you who hear me: Love your enemies, do good to those who hate you, bless those who curse you, pray for those who mistreat you. If someone strikes you on one cheek, turn to him the other also. If someone takes your cloak, do not stop him from taking your tunic. Give to everyone who asks you, and if anyone takes what belongs to you, do not demand it back. Do to others as you would have them do to you.
>
> If you love those who love you, what credit is that to you? Even "sinners" love those who love them. And if you do good to those who are good to you, what credit is that to you? Even "sinners" do that. And if you lend to those from whom you expect repayment, what credit is that to you? Even "sinners" lend to "sinners," expecting to be repaid in full. But love your enemies, do good to them, and lend to them without expecting to get anything back. Then your reward will be great, and you will be sons of the Most High, because he is kind to the ungrateful and wicked. Be merciful, just as your Father is merciful.

As figure 8 indicates, this passage outlines a comprehensive plan for Christlike ministry to those who mistreat us.

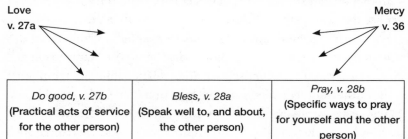

Figure 8. The Luke 6:27–36 game plan for ministering to unrepentant offenders

Do good, v. 27b (Practical acts of service for the other person)	Bless, v. 28a (Speak well to, and about, the other person)	Pray, v. 28b (Specific ways to pray for yourself and the other person)

We begin with two mega-words that frame our unit like a pair of bookends: "love" (v. 27a) and "mercy" (v. 36). These two Spirit-produced graces represent two overarching attitudes that God wants us to have toward our enemies. They result from grasping how God in Christ has loved us and shown us mercy (Luke 7:36–50; 18:9–14; Rom. 5:6–11; Eph. 2:1–10; 5:1–2; and Titus 3:4–7). To love our enemies is a central tenet of Jesus's teaching, one he modeled in his graciousness toward critics and crucifiers, in his washing the feet of his betrayer Judas, and in his sacrificial death for us while we were his enemies. Developing this attitude involves soaking our minds in the cross of Christ and asking God to make our hearts loving and merciful toward the offender.

In Luke 6:27b–28 we see three specific ministries that reflect Christlike love and mercy: "Do good to those who hate you, bless those who curse you, pray for those who mistreat you." The remaining verses in the unit, verses 29–35, give further examples of these three basic ministries.

Let's consider each of these ministries, including some questions to help you brainstorm some specific action steps under each heading.

1. Do good. In verse 27b, Jesus says, "Do good to those who hate you," and in the ensuing verses he gives us some examples. In Romans 12:17–21, in light of God's saving mercy to us in Christ (v. 1), the apostle Paul gives similar counsel.

> Do not repay anyone evil for evil. Be careful to do what is right in the eyes of everybody. If it is possible, as far as it depends on you, live at peace with everyone. Do not take revenge, my friends, but leave room for God's wrath, for it is written: "It is mine to avenge; I will repay," says the Lord. On the contrary:
>
> > "If your enemy is hungry, feed him;
> >   if he is thirsty, give him something to drink.
> > In doing this, you will heap burning coals on his head."
>
> Do not be overcome by evil, but overcome evil with good.

Like his Lord Jesus, Paul calls us to overcome the evil of others by doing good to them, even to the point of feeding them.

Jesus furnishes a dramatic example in John 13:1–5. John sets the scene in the upper room, where Jesus is alone with his twelve disciples: "It was just before the Passover Feast. . . . The evening meal was being served, and the devil had already prompted Judas Iscariot, son of Simon, to betray Jesus" (vv. 1–2). Jesus then swung into action.

> Jesus knew that the Father had put all things under his power, and that he had come from God and was returning to God; so he got up from the meal, took off his outer clothing, and wrapped a towel around his waist. After that, he poured water into a basin and began to wash his disciples' feet, drying them with the towel that was wrapped around him. (vv. 3–5)

Whose feet did Jesus wash? The chronology in the four Gospels suggests that Judas was still present and that Jesus knew Judas was about to betray him. If you had in your hands the ankle of the man who was about to betray you into the hands of your murderers, what would you do with it? I know what my own temptation would be! Yet Jesus chose to wash Judas's feet, mercifully displaying his love and giving Judas still another opportunity to repent.

By the way, there is a strong lesson here for us. Jesus's service sprang from his clear sense of his identity before his Father. As he grabbed the towel, Jesus knew three things: (1) that "the Father had put all things under his power," (2) that "he had come from God," and (3) that he "was returning to God" (v. 3). In other words, Jesus's identity, origin, and destiny were all secured by God his Father. And based on that—note the "so" in verse 4, "so he got up"—Jesus could show kindness to his betrayer. Only a secure identity in Christ—as a son or daughter of the living God—will allow you to do good to those who oppose you.

What does this look like in your situation? What good deeds can you do for that person who has betrayed you? How can you display Christlike kindness by serving him in specific ways? It begins with refraining from vengeful actions—not repaying evil for evil. Yet it also includes positive actions. It may mean sending a birthday card or dropping off a present or a dessert to your separated spouse. It may mean continuing to patronize the offender's business establishment or covering part of your coworker's heavy workload. As you reflect on God's Word, seek godly counsel, and pray for wisdom, don't be surprised if God shows you some practical, creative ways to show his love and mercy to that person who hurt you.

2. Bless. Jesus continues in Luke 6:28a with a call to "bless those who curse you." To bless someone means to desire for him God's favor and to speak well to him and about him. How might you control your speech when speaking *to* the offender? How might you control your speech when speaking to others *about* the offender? Reviewing the passages about godly speech in chapter 11 ("Ministry Strategy 2," including godly listening) will help you; most of the passages apply equally to our conversations with friends or with enemies.

Two verses in Proverbs seem especially helpful amid tense relationships.

> Reckless words pierce like a sword,
>> but the tongue of the wise brings healing. (Prov. 12:18)

> A gentle answer turns away wrath,
>> but a harsh word stirs up anger. (Prov. 15:1)

But in many ways Peter's description of Jesus sets the standard for self-controlled speech in the face of mistreatment.

> To this you were called, because Christ suffered for you, leaving you an example, that you should follow in his steps.
>
> "He committed no sin,
> and no deceit was found in his mouth."
>
> When they hurled their insults at him, he did not retaliate; when he suffered, he made no threats. Instead, he entrusted himself to him who judges justly. (1 Pet. 2:21–23)

But it goes beyond that. How can you bless—speak well to and speak well about—the other person with your words (written, oral, posted, or e-mailed)? What will you say to him? What will you say about him to others? How can you speak with edifying speech?

3. Pray. Luke 6:28 concludes with our third ministry toward our enemies, or those who act like them: "pray for those who mistreat you." This includes praying for the offender's repentance, that God would work directly and mightily in his life and use various means and agents to draw him to the Lord. But this also can remind us to pray for ourselves—to ask God to give us a heart of love and mercy, to help us better apply his Word, to give us wisdom to know what to do and not to do to minister well to the other person, and to use this hardship to make us more like Jesus. And we can pray for others who are involved—asking God to care for them, to use this hardship to draw them closer to the Lord, and to help them minister wisely to you and the offender. God sometimes uses a third party to bring together unreconciled people.

How can you pray for yourself right now? How can you pray for the other person? What can you ask God to be doing in you and in others? Consider also Luke 11:5–13; Romans 10:1; and Ephesians 3:14–21.

From your brainstormed lists in all three columns of figure 8, with the counsel of your advisors, you can select concrete action steps to show God's love and mercy to the person who remains unreconciled with you.

The Lord used this Luke 6 game plan to help Angie deal with her sister Kathy. Three years ago Angie accidentally told their mom some information about Kathy that Kathy had confided with Angie. Their mom shared the information with Kathy, and as soon as they hung up, Kathy—enraged—called Angie to confront her. Angie pursued peace according to the truths in our previous chapters, but Kathy remained cold and unforgiving. As Angie and I talked, it became evident that she had sincerely, humbly, and diligently sought peace with Kathy, but Kathy refused. To apply the model, Angie first focused on God's grace in her own life. One particular truth in Luke 6 overwhelmed her: God is "kind to the ungrateful and wicked" (v. 35). Angie recognized not only this sin against her sister but a dozen others in different areas of her life. Yet God was loving and merciful—"kind to the ungrateful and wicked." God's Spirit was inclining Angie's heart to be merciful to her spiteful sister.

Angie's "Do good" action steps included sending Kathy and her children occasional gifts and electronic greeting cards. She also offered to let Kathy's children visit her for a week or two in the summer. The category of "Bless" proved a bit more difficult, but the Lord helped her. She found it especially difficult to control her tongue when their brother Don expressed to Angie his similar frustrations with Kathy. On some occasions Angie had to confront Don about his sinful venting about Kathy. Angie also learned to overlook some rude comments that Kathy made to her at their parents' house at Thanksgiving. She was conscious of her Lord's stance in 1 Peter 2:23: "When they hurled their insults at him, he did not retaliate; when he suffered, he made no threats."

Lastly, based on the "Pray" column, Angie wrote several prayer requests on a 3" × 5" card and began to pray these each morning. She prayed for Kathy: "Lord, I don't know what's going on in her relationship with you, but please draw near to her and help her to connect well to you." "Father, please melt Kathy's bitterness, not just for my sake but for her sake—it's eating her up—and for her husband's sake, her children's sake, and your sake." Angie also prayed for herself: "Father, help me to show love and mercy to my sister." "Lord, give me wisdom when I am around Mom and Dad and Kathy so that I would know what to say, especially if Kathy treats me rudely." She also recognized the danger of giving up completely, of ignoring God's power to ever change her sister. As we saw in chapter 3, such pessimism discounts God's power to change people: to mentally consign a now-hardened person to an entire lifetime of hard-heartedness betrays nothing less than unbelief in God's mighty, merciful hand. Therefore, Angie prayed, "Father, help me not to become hardened in my heart and fail to pray for Kathy. Help me not to presume that you will change her or demand that you must, but help me also never to forget that you can change her and never to stop asking you to do so."

Ministry Strategy 5: Keep a God-Centered, Balanced Perspective for Your Life

The last ministry step takes us, in one sense, full circle, back to where we began with ministry step 1, keeping our relationship with the Lord central. It is also an excellent theme on which to conclude this book. Here the balance is to pursue peace in conflicted relationships (as the entire book has urged) without forgetting our big-picture focus on God and without neglecting our calling also to serve other people and carry out our other responsibilities.

Three passages of Scripture will keep us from becoming overly consumed with the person who has wronged us. In Psalm 62:3–4 David reports enemy threats. Yet in the midst of evil people he urges us to find our rest in God.

> Find rest, O my soul, in God alone;
> my hope comes from him.
> He alone is my rock and my salvation;
> he is my fortress, I will not be shaken.
> My salvation and my honor depend on God;
> he is my mighty rock, my refuge.
> Trust in him at all times, O people;
> pour out your hearts to him,
> for God is our refuge. (vv. 5–8)

Amid your unreconciled relationships, rest your soul—alone—in your Rock and Salvation.

Consider Psalm 73, in which the writer testifies in the opening stanzas of his near apostasy from God and then summarizes the solid truths that secured his soul.

Yet I am always with you;
    you hold me by my right hand.
You guide me with your counsel,
    and afterward you will take me into glory.
Whom have I in heaven but you?
    And earth has nothing I desire besides you.
My flesh and my heart may fail,
    but God is the strength of my heart
    and my portion forever.

Those who are far from you will perish;
    you destroy all who are unfaithful to you.
But as for me, it is good to be near God.
    I have made the Sovereign LORD my refuge;
    I will tell of all your deeds. (vv. 23–28)

The most important relationship for the psalmist is his intimate connection with the Lord. His highest good is not relational reconciliation with a spouse or friend but being near to his all-sufficient God.

Lastly, there is Paul's remarkable buoyancy and balance in Philippians 4:11–13. As one who has experienced an array of circumstantial ups and downs, the apostle declares, "I have learned to be content whatever the circumstances. I know what it is to be in need, and I know what it is to have plenty. I have learned the secret of being content in any and every situation, whether well fed or hungry, whether living in plenty or in want" (vv. 11–12). While Paul's situation in this text involves financial hardships, I believe that with God's help we can apply the same principle to relational struggles. In other words, we can paraphrase Paul: "I have learned to be content whatever my relationships. I know what it is to be mistreated, and I know what it is to be loved by others. I have learned the secret of being content in any and every relationship, whether it's reconciled or unreconciled, whether living in peace or in conflict."

How can we ever learn this kind of contentment when we suffer the loss of unreconciled relationships? The same way Paul learned contentment—from the Lord: "I can do everything through him who gives me strength" (Phil. 4:13). The promise is not about becoming spiritual supermen or superwomen who will accomplish spectacular feats for God. It's about learning by faith how to face hard circumstances—including wrecked relationships—in ways that demonstrate dependence on the Lord, seek the power he provides, and live out our identity as God's sons and daughters.

> Blessed are the peacemakers,
> for they will be called sons of God. (Matt. 5:9)

For Personal Reflection or Group Discussion

1. Reflect on an unreconciled relationship that you currently experience. Review the five ministry strategies above and select one that would be most helpful to focus on at this point.

2. Select one or more of the following unreconciled relationships a Christian might have, or supply one of your own, and discuss what a concrete Luke 6:27–36 game plan might look like:

   a. A Christian trying to have a workable, civil shared-parenting relationship with his or her angry ex-spouse.
   b. A Christian trying to minister to someone who has been excommunicated from his church.
   c. A Christian trying to handle his boss when the boss has mistreated him and not admitted it or sought to make things right.

APPENDIX A

Forgiveness on Two Levels

What Others Say

In chapter 8 I presented a two-level approach to understanding forgiveness as both unconditional and conditional. I called Level 1 attitudinal forgiveness, heart forgiveness, or dispositional forgiveness. I called Level 2 transacted forgiveness, granted forgiveness, or relational forgiveness. We must always forgive any offender attitudinally; we should grant forgiveness only to those who repent.

How do biblical counselors understand this dual-forgiveness dynamic? I believe this twofold approach best encompasses the whole of Scripture, including texts that seemingly emphasize one or the other side of the tension without draining them of their meaning. As we saw in chapter 8, this approach allows us to reconcile the apparent unconditional command to forgive in Mark 11 and Jesus's prayer in Luke 24 with the conditional components in Luke 17 and Acts 2. The former relates to a kind of forgiveness that I commit to hold in my heart; the second allows full reconciliation when repentance occurs.

To some extent, most leading writers on biblical counseling subscribe to some version of this twofold forgiveness, albeit with varying terminology:

- Paul David Tripp calls the two levels "judicial forgiveness" and "relational forgiveness," and he sequences them in the same way as above.[1]
- Jay E. Adams (in his early writings) summarizes the above twofold distinction this way: "Forgiveness is *granted* to another only when he seeks it, but internally one forgives (i.e., he no longer holds on to the offense as something that could turn to bitterness) in his heart in prayer (Mark 11:25)."[2] Based on this distinction, Adams might

---

[1] Paul David Tripp, *War of Words: Getting to the Heart of Your Communication Struggles* (Phillipsburg, NJ: P&R, 2000), 240–43.
[2] Jay E. Adams, *Ready to Restore: A Layman's Guide to Christian Counseling* (Phillipsburg, NJ: Presbyterian and Reformed, 1981), 84, emphasis his. See also his *A Theology of*

call our two levels "internal" and "granted." He agrees that there is a kind of internal heart forgiveness that we must give even if there is no repentance.

- Ken Sande distinguishes between his promise 1 ("I will not dwell on your offense"), which we make toward all offenders, and his promises 2–4, which we make toward repentant offenders. Sande speaks of attitudinal and granted forgiveness as two stages.[3]
- Alfred Poirier also refers to the two levels as two stages: dispositional and transactional. Poirier even suggests that God's election of believers prior to our conversion parallels God's dispositional forgiveness.[4]
- Tim Lane teaches this same twofold approach that I've presented.[5]

Some speakers use still other terminology to capture the twofold dynamic. I recall hearing one teacher describe our Level 1—citing Mark 11:25—as "pre-forgiveness" or a "willingness to forgive," and our Level 2 as "forgiveness." The downside of this, however, is that in Mark 11:25 Jesus calls this first level "forgiveness," not "pre-forgiveness." Later I heard another speaker call the first "forgiveness" and the second "reconciliation." But in Luke 17:3–4 Jesus calls the second idea "forgiveness." Two respected Bible teachers with the same essential twofold view were using the same Bible term with two differing meanings! Rather than calling one forgiveness and the other pre-forgiveness, or calling one forgiveness and the other reconciliation, I prefer to call them both forgiveness, *as the Bible does*, but to distinguish them with the above adjectives according to sequenced levels or stages. In other words, it seems safer to resolve the apparent tension between Bible passages by adding clarifying adjectives like *attitudinal* or *transacted* than to remove the word *forgiveness* itself.

Christian Counseling: More Than Redemption (1979; Grand Rapids: Zondervan, 1986), 230. However, in one of his subsequent books, *From Forgiven to Forgiving: Discovering the Path to Biblical Forgiveness* (Wheaton, IL: Victor, 1989), 34–36, Adams argues that the word *forgiveness* is only used conditionally, interpreting Mark 11:25 as "ready" to forgive (although he recognizes, of course, the biblical call to get rid of bitterness).

[3]Ken Sande, *The Peacemaker: A Biblical Guide to Resolving Personal Conflict*, 3rd ed. (Grand Rapids: Baker, 2004), 210–11.

[4]Alfred Poirier, *The Peacemaking Pastor: A Biblical Guide to Resolving Church Conflict* (Grand Rapids: Baker, 2006), 155–57.

[5]Timothy S. Lane, *Forgiving Others: Joining Wisdom and Love* (Greensboro, NC: New Growth, 2005), 15–16.

What advantages do we gain by taking this twofold approach? On the level of theory, I believe this approach better captures the Bible's language of forgiveness. Books on forgiveness that stress either conditional or unconditional forgiveness often fail to address carefully the most important passages. Our approach allows us to see more clearly the Bible's own nuances. It also allows us to understand and to engage those who hold to popular evangelical notions that all forgiveness is to be unconditional, that we are to tell the unrepentant person that we forgive him, and so on. We can concur with them in part, as I explain in the left column of table 1 above, but we can then encourage them to consider the unbiblical nature of forgetting the right column, ignoring the presence of sin, discarding justice, enabling evil behavior, and the like.

On the practical level, maintaining the distinction between attitudinal and granted forgiveness gives us a clear path on how to view and treat the offender. Without this guidance, confusion and uncertainties can remain. Should I forgive, or shouldn't I? I can feel guilty—a distorted, twisted guilt—if I haven't forgiven him, but letting him go scot-free seems wrong as well. If I forgive an unrepentant person, I may be tolerating and enabling further sin. Therefore, our dual distinction clears the confusion by providing two distinct strategies, depending on whether the offender is repentant or not.

APPENDIX B

I Believe in the Forgiveness of Sins

A Meditation on God's Forgiveness through Christ's Cross

"I believe in the forgiveness of sins." That simple sentence from the ancient Apostles' Creed has summarized the faith of millions of Christians for nearly two millennia.

"I believe in the forgiveness of sins." Why? On what basis can sinners like me and you—people who have failed to obey God fully—ever hope to have our many sins forgiven?

We find the answer in the cross of Jesus Christ. The Bible says, "In him we have redemption through his blood, the forgiveness of sins, in accordance with the riches of God's grace" (Eph. 1:7; also Col. 1:13–14). God's forgiveness comes through the blood of his Son—his violent, self-sacrificing death as our substitute. Our forgiveness is wrapped up in our Redeemer.

What does it mean to be forgiven? Simply this: Based on Jesus's death, God has decided, declared, and promised to not hold our sins against us. God has decided, declared, and promised to release us from our debt against him, to not charge us with our guilt, to lift the liability we have incurred, and to remove the penalty our sins deserve.

How does Jesus's death do this? The God who decided to not hold our sins against us did decide to hold our sins against his own Son. In other words, all our sins must be punished; each deserves judgment and death. God cannot maintain his holy purity and simply overlook them. So what did God do? He did bring punishment for our sins, but not on us, but on Jesus our substitute. As 1 Peter puts it, "He himself bore our sins in his body on the tree. . . . For Christ died for sins once for all, the righteous for the unrighteous, to bring you to God" (1 Pet. 2:24; 3:18a).

The Old Testament predicted the forgiveness Christ would purchase. The book of Hebrews tells us that Jesus has now fulfilled Jeremiah's new covenant promise.

> For I will forgive their wickedness
>> and will remember their sins no more. (Heb. 8:12; Jer. 31:34)

Later in the same book Jeremiah looked forward again to that day.

> "In those days, at that time,"
>> declares the LORD,
> "search will be made for Israel's guilt,
>> but there will be none,
> and for the sins of Judah,
>> but none will be found,
>> for I will forgive the remnant I spare." (Jer. 50:20)

Why will God not find the sins of his people? Because on that one Good Friday, God indeed *did* find our sins—not on us, but on our substitute, Jesus, slain for us.

My friend, do you wallow in your sins? Do you struggle with self-recrimination? Do you wrestle with accusations from others, or from your conscience, or from the Devil? Jesus's words to all who trust in him are plain: "Son [or daughter], your sins are forgiven" (Mark 2:5; Luke 7:48). Instead of the endless drip, drip, drip of guilt, God now showers you with forgiveness. His promises of daily grace cascade upon you like a brisk cool fountain.

What are his promises? By faith, listen to God's Word to you: "I have removed your sins as far as the east is from the west. Though they were like scarlet, I have made them white as snow. I have put all your sins behind my back. I, even I, am he who blots out your transgressions, and remembers your sins no more. I have swept away your offenses like a cloud, your sins like the morning mist. I have tread them underfoot and hurled them into the ocean depths" (see Ps. 103:12; Isa. 1:18; 38:17; 43:25; 44:22; Mic. 7:19).

"I believe in the forgiveness of sins." Do you?

General Index

rejected by men, 139
return of, 40
served others, 168–69
as substitute, 101–2, 126
washing feet of Judas, 189
journal-keeping, 119
joy, 21, 24
judgment, 76n1, 134, 143–44
of God, 21
judgmentalism, 80, 144
judicial forgiveness, 196
justice, 99, 127, 145, 158, 185–86
justification, 49

keeping score, of wrongs, 163
Kennedy, D. James, 145
kindness, 112–13, 188
kind words, 175

Lane, Tim, 197
lawsuits, 186n3
legalism, 77
Lewis, C. S., 122, 123
license, 77
life change, 164
like-mindedness, 176, 178
listening, 161
love, 41, 44, 116, 117–18
for enemies, 187–88
for God, 19, 32, 85
for neighbor, 19, 32, 85
and rebuke, 151, 159
Lucas, Dick, 107–8

marriage conflict, 17, 31–33
means of grace, 88
memories, of offense, 162
Merchant of Venice (Shakespeare), 144
mercy, 41, 112, 143–44, 189
ministry, tailored to specific people, 170–71
moralism, 60

need
for God's mercy, 143–44
for God's forgiveness, 142–43
new covenant, 126, 130
new heart, 63
new life, 108

obedience, 47, 49. *See also* pleasing God
offenses, identification of, 83–85
omission sins, 77–78

opportunity, conflict as, 37–42
others-centeredness, 170n1, 176–77, 178
overlooking, versus rebuking sin, 153–54

Packer, J. I., 110
parable of the Pharisee and the tax collector, 80
parable of the unforgiving servant, 139–41
parent-child relationship, 33–34
patience, 114–15, 118
pattern of sin, 156
Paul
contentment of, 194–95
self-sacrificial ministry of, 177
Peacemaker Ministries, 95
people pleasing, 47, 160
perseverance
in conflicts, 32
in unreconciled relationships, 187
Philippians, as peacemaking book, 176–77
plank sins, 76–78, 83–85, 87, 91, 92, 159
versus specks, 81–82
pleasing God, 43–56, 104, 160, 183–84
"Pleasing God Prayer," 54–55
pleasing oneself, 47
pleasing others, 47
Poirier, Alfred, 156n1, 197
prayer, 50, 119
for unrepentant offenders, 188, 191–93
pre-forgiveness, 197
private contact with offender, 160
procrastination, in handling conflict, 155
"Progression of an Idol," 64–65
progressive sanctification, 88, 102
promises of God, 200
Proverbs, 52

racism, 135
radical service, 170n1
rage, 157
rebellion, 146–48
rebuke, 151–66
recognizing, desires becoming demands, 66–67
reconciliation, 21, 32, 135, 159–60
and deepening of friendship, 165
through pleasing God, 51–53
record of wrongs, 163
redemption of situations, 38
refocus, 70–72
relational forgiveness. *See* transacted forgiveness
relational graces, 72, 116–18

Scripture Index

205